Social Mobility in the English Bildungsroman

Gissing, Hardy, Bennett, and Lawrence

Studies in Modern Literature, No. 58

A. Walton Litz, General Series Editor

Professor of English
Princeton University

Keith Cushman

Consulting Editor for Titles on D.H. Lawrence
Professor of English
University of North Carolina at Greensboro

Other Titles in This Series

Social Mobility in the English Bildungsroman

Gissing, Hardy, Bennett, and Lawrence

by
Patricia Alden

UMI RESEARCH PRESS

Ann Arbor, Michigan

Produced and distributed by
UMI Research Press
an imprint of
University Microfilms, Inc.
Ann Arbor, Michigan 48106

Library of Congress Cataloging in Publication Data

Alden, Patricia, 1945-
  Social mobility in the English Bildungsroman.

  (Studies in modern literature ; no. 58)
  "A revision of the author's Ph. D. thesis,
Stanford University, 1979"—T.p. verso.
  Bibliography: p.
  Includes index.
  1. English fiction—19th century—History and
criticism. 2. Social classes in literature. 3. Social
mobility in literature. 4. Bildungsroman.
  5. Lawrence, D.H. (David Herbert), 1885-1930—
Political and social views. I. Title. II. Series.
PR878.S6A44 1986   823'.09355   86-7050
ISBN 0-8357-1740-2 (alk. paper)

For A. N. A. and R. H. A.

Contents

Acknowledgments

In the course of writing this book I have benefited from the counsel and encouragement of many people. I would thank, first, Wilfred Stone, George Dekker, and Robert Carlisle, each of whom helped me to gain insight into literary history and criticism. The Mrs. Giles Whiting Foundation provided a fellowship which allowed me to travel to England. The library staffs at Stanford University and St. Lawrence University, in particular Margaret Guccione and Jennifer Knapp, have been generous with their assistance. My thanks to Keith Cushman for recommending my work to UMI Research Press, and to St. Lawrence for financial assistance in preparing the manuscript.

One's greatest debts are also the most difficult to define. The stimulation of colleagues from graduate school, at St. Lawrence, and at the Culture and Society summer conferences has proved invaluable both in the examples of scholarly endeavor and in the encouragement given me. My husband's loving support has never faltered. Perhaps my most incalculable debt is to my uncle, Donald Alden, through whom I am fruitfully haunted by the past.

Portions of chapters 2 and 3 have been published in revised form in *The Gissing Newsletter* (Vol. 17, no. 3, July 1981) and in *The Colby Library Quarterly* (Vol. 19, no. 1, March 1983). My thanks to both journals for permission to use this material. I am also grateful to Macmillan Publishers for their excellent editions of Hardy. For permission to use the photographs, I thank the Thomas Hardy Memorial Collection in the Dorset County Museum, Dorchester; the National Portrait Gallery, London; and the British Library. For permission to use material from *Phoenix* and from *The Letters of D. H. Lawrence,* I thank The Estate of Mrs. Frieda Lawrence Ravagli and Laurence Polliger Ltd. For permission to use material from other works by Lawrence, my thanks to Viking Penguin, Inc.

Introduction

The Bildungsroman: Genre and Ideology

From its beginnings the English novel was the favored child of the rising middle class, which grasped how well suited this form was to representing, and so giving value to, the experience of individuals. The business of daily life, the commonly shared milestones of marriages, births, deaths and inheritances and, above all, the new experience of social mobility which allowed ordinary people to plot their own trajectory in the social world became the material for fiction. New ideas about the worth of ordinary men and women and the legitimacy of social mobility thus had found a literary voice, and nowhere more so than in the Bildungsroman, or novel of formation. The term of course was borrowed from German and referred to a genre regularly associated with Goethe's *Wilhelm Meister's Apprenticeship* (1795-96), a genre that has proved difficult to define.[1] I shall use Bildungsroman to refer to a kind of novel which flourished in France and England as well as in Germany in the eighteenth and nineteenth centuries and which includes such novels as *Sentimental Education, Lost Illusions, Great Expectations,* and *The Ordeal of Richard Feveral.* The genre focuses on the development of a single individual within a particular social world; it may be in part autobiographical; it is likely to give the history of this individual from childhood up to a point at which the development or unfolding of his or her character is achieved; in other words it is the story of apprenticeship rather than a life history. Central to the genre is the notion of individual selfhood achieved through growth and of social experience as an education which forms, and sometimes deforms, that self. The projected resolution of this process is some kind of adjustment to society. Wherever it appeared, the Bildungsroman was associated with bourgeois humanism, with faith in progress and with the value of the individual.

Defined this way, we recognize that the Bildungsroman was among the earliest types of novel in England. It readily accommodated the concerns of a new middle-class reading public, willing to be absorbed by the history of an individual and gratified to see how its collective experience of social mobility might be rendered as the individual's pursuit of an ideal of self-development. In its English form, then, the Bildungsroman linked the individual's moral, spiritual, and psychological maturation with his economic and social advancement. Certain material conditions were presumed to be prerequisites for the expansion of sensibility and intellect. Early examples of the genre ended with the individual's assimilation to an aristocratic or genteel elite which represented an ideal standard of cultivation. Not only did the Bildungsroman legitimate the experience of upward mobility, it also instructed the middle class in how to accomplish it.

In his introduction to *Henry Esmond,* G. Robert Stange notes how readily the experience of social mobility could be grafted on to this genre.

> The pattern of the Bildungsroman is peculiarly suited to its time.... such a novel is, among other things, a guide to the good life. In outline... the Bildungsroman is almost an image of the life of the middle class. Novels of all kinds depend on some kind of movement, but the difference between the journey in the relatively primitive picaresque novel and the progression in the Bildungsroman is that in the latter, movement is vertical; the hero does not merely travel about the world, he develops, he rises in society, he advances toward intellectual, moral, and economic goals. The form is very much the creation of an age dominated by ideas of evolutionary progress, and for novelists wracked by a sense of rapid and devastating change it provided a way of registering social mobility and recording its effects on the plastic sensibility of the hero.[2]

This vertical movement and the assimilation of economic, social, and moral improvements are apparent in Samuel Richardson's *Pamela* (1740). Writing from a solidly bourgeois perspective, Richardson presents Pamela's upward mobility less as development than as an appropriate material reward for her virtue, affirming that the union of a serving girl and an aristocrat will be mutually enriching. But Henry Fielding and later Jane Austen, both with some connections to a landed gentry, probe more deeply the development of their protagonists' minds and hearts, their sense and sensibility, showing how they are prepared by their experience to assume a place within a social elite. In *Tom Jones* (1749), *Pride and Prejudice* (1813), and others of their novels, Fielding and Austen seek to educate a rising class in a standard of culture identified with a landed ruling class. Neither writer questions the assumption that material goods and superior social station enhance our ability to realize our full human potential. For them the ideal of human cultivation is naturally represented by those social ranks which have long enjoyed material advantages. Individual development depends on the maintenance of a particular social order while requiring that newcomers be able to move up into it. Both writers are confident that their ideal of cultivation can be extended and preserved if social mobility continues "with all deliberate speed"; self and society, bourgeoisie and aristocracy, may be successfully, if slowly, integrated.

However, in the course of the nineteenth century this sanguine view of social mobility is not sustained by most major writers, and the fundamentally comic form of the Bildungsroman becomes problematic, satiric, or tragic. We can see this happening in the 1840s in the fiction of Charlotte Brontë, whose vulnerable social situation enables her to present the experience of social mobility as a hardship to be carefully negotiated by her hard-pressed heroines. Their development is a matter of winning through this battle some kind of inner harmony; their integration into an appropriate social world remains in question, as the endings of *Jane Eyre* and *Villette* both make clear in different ways.[3]

The political crises of 1848 provide an appropriate point from which to date the increasingly disillusioned view of both society and the individual's potential for meaningful development within it. The promise of bourgeois individualism has led to Boffin's dustheaps and his ethic of "scrunch or be scrunched." Thackeray's *Vanity Fair* gives us a satirical inversion of the Bildungsroman, pointing to the impossibility of combining bourgeois individualism and genuine cultivation. The society to which Becky aspires is revealed, through her apt mimicry, to be as spurious as she; individual and society are perfectly harmonized in their mutual inauthenticity. By 1860 Dickens's great Bildungsroman, *Great Expectations,* depicts a world in which money has usurped the place of genuine value and cultivation. Upward mobility which formerly led to freedom and self-development now leads only to alienation and moral compromise, to a "Vanity Fair" in which money counts for everything but can buy nothing of value. The only way out is down. While this affords a satisfactory resolution to the moral fable, issues relevant to the Bildungsroman remain unresolved; hence, Dickens leaves Pip not at the forge but working in the colonies, at the margins of capital, still lured on by the cultivation which Estella, for all the taint that is on her, continues to represent.[4]

Novelists in the latter half of the nineteenth century increasingly assume an inevitable, unbridgeable estrangement between society and any youth capable of cultivation. The hero is often an artist manqué, and his development is a lonely, internal process which sometimes ends in his death. George Meredith's *The Ordeal of Richard Feveral,* Walter Pater's *Marius the Epicurean,* Samuel Butler's *The Way of All Flesh,* and Henry James's *The Princess Casamassima* are landmark works contrasting the inherent refinement of the hero's sensibility with the crass world which affords it no home. In these works inner cultivation has become so separated from economic and social rise that either the protagonist's upward mobility has become irrelevant or, as in James, esthetic and moral sensibility are completely split, the former nurtured by the country house, the latter by revolution.

In its early form the Bildungsroman was well suited to serve the interests of its bourgeois audience. By celebrating the individual's potential for development and by projecting a final harmony between self and society, it promised a sunny end to an economic revolution. But as it developed, the genre came increasingly to expose contradictions in the ideology of individualism. While the individual's desire for self-development might be approved, this value could not be extended to a class without inviting the usurpation of the established order which defined what culture was in the first instance and whose material base made that standard realizable. Moreover, the social and political order brought into being by the new ideology was so unacceptable that the individual could only shun it and retreat into himself, flying as a lonely standard the slogan "Long live individualism." The problem of how that self was to be nurtured in its isolation from material goods and social intercourse remained unsolved.

*   *   *

The contradictions discovered in the Bildungsroman were particularly acute for the four writers included in this study. Throughout the nineteenth century opportunities for social mobility had increased, and with them new pressure to rise and, concomitantly, a loss in the value of rising. In Matthew Arnold's world of Barbarians, Philistines, and Populace, movement up the social ladder could no longer be seen as an appropriate path toward self-development. Coming from the lower-middle or working classes, deprived of easy access to education and material support, Gissing, Hardy, Bennett, and Lawrence knew intimately the pressure to rise and the value of bourgeois security. As petty bourgeois, they felt particularly pressed to take advantage of the new opportunities for upward mobility or risk slipping down into a growing proletariat. Yet to move up was in some sense to betray the past, the community of one's roots, the innocent self. Moreover, to move up was to be tainted, compromised by association with grasping *nouveaux riches,* with *arrivistes,* and with a social transformation they deplored.

These writers felt themselves to be in a double bind in which success or failure in upward mobility equally precluded the possibility for cultivation of the whole person. This double bind becomes a characteristic feature of their semi-autobiographical Bildungsromane: *Born in Exile, Jude the Obscure, Clayhanger, Sons and Lovers,* and *The Rainbow.* These are significant reworkings of the Bildungsroman which had projected the harmonious integration of the individual into a social and material culture supportive of his development. Instead these writers find only the possibility of self-betrayal which leads to disintegration of self, an overwhelming sense of the powerlessness of the individual to effect his development, and a complete rupture between self and society. In their work the issue of social mobility is addressed with new urgency and new sensitivity, for the need to rise cannot be ignored, the urgent demands of the self cannot be met with a fable. Nor can they escape from society and develop the self in solitude, for the need for appropriate material conditions is urgent for these writers. The double bind motif points to contradictions in liberal ideology, contradictions which are repressed by the writers but which energize their exploration.[5]

Historical Background: Class, Culture, and Social Mobility

At the end of the eighteenth century England was still a largely agrarian society of distinct estates or ranks, within which the landed aristocracy and gentry together maintained a widely approved standard of cultivation. During the nineteenth century, as the industrial and democratic revolutions gained momentum, the centuries-old, hierarchical caste system was displaced by a highly stratified but fluid class structure in which an individual's social position was increasingly determined not by birth but by bank account and occupation.[6] The roots of this social transformation reach back into the eighteenth century, but the 1832 Reform Bill, extending the franchise to a small portion of the middle class, inaugurated a period of gradual change in the social and political structure during which the landowning aristocracy and gentry made common cause with the new classes associated with industrial expansion and commercial enterprise. Over several decades a new upper-middle-class elite was forged, to a very considerable extent in the public schools and universities.

The shift from an agrarian to an industrial economy assured England's continued economic growth; it became the leading manufacturing nation in the world and expanded its empire overseas. This prosperity spurred the creation of new occupations and social roles and fostered an unprecedented degree of social mobility. Careers opened up in the civil service and local government, in engineering, architecture, law, medicine, education and research, journalism, and a variety of businesses, all these positions commanding increasing public esteem and social standing as the century wore on. The increase in social mobility created new pressure to rise, both because of the "carrot" of higher status and because of the "stick" of failure to make something of one's self. Mobility was not really a choice when "standing still" amounted to slipping down into the working class. Certainly the new possibilities for mobility helped to legitimate the ideology of individualism: a man could rise through his own exertions; he had control over his destiny.

These new opportunities put pressure on the educational system in England. If careers were to be open to men of talent, they needed training, often in new fields. And democracy, though it came ever so slowly, nevertheless required an educated populace. Throughout the century the need for more schooling at the primary, secondary, and university levels was addressed in a variety of ways. Efforts to insure universal education at the primary level culminated in the passage of the 1870 Education Act, which came, it is worth noting, in the wake of the 1867 extension of the franchise. In the 1850s and 1860s Parliament established three commissions to review the universities, public schools, and endowed secondary schools. Reforms included some liberalization of the curricula to include more science and mathematics in order to better provide for an industrially-based economy and emphasis on competitive examination for entrance into school and university and into such professions as the civil service. The ancient universities began to get some competition when in 1832 the University of London was founded, and by the 1850s provincial universities such as Owens College in Manchester, which Gissing attended, were helping to meet the need for expanded university education.

Despite all this expansion and the efforts of some to make education accessible and equal on a competitive basis, the reality was that the education system was *the* important brake on upward mobility, the chief means of preserving hierarchy in a developing political democracy. To accumulate money in that burgeoning economy was comparatively simple, but to acquire the manners, tastes, and accent of a gentleman was a more delicate task. The sons of manufacturers and captains of industry and commerce pressed to enter the old public schools and the universities where they might be educated in customs, values, and social vision appropriate to their new station. In his history of British education in the nineteenth century, Brian Simon argues that educational reforms were carefully managed by the new ruling class coalition in order to maintain class distinctions and to preserve privilege. "In the period 1850–70 a conscious effort was made to establish a closed system of schools; so to divide and differentiate the education given to different social classes that privilege could for ever withstand the pressure of the working masses." This was achieved by establishing clearly differentiated tracks at the secondary level, with a curriculum for each appropriate to the class it was designed to serve.[7]

While the theory of an educational ladder was preserved, the reality was that many reforms worked to make that ladder very narrow indeed. For instance the Royal Commission appointed in 1850 to recommend reforms at Oxford, Cambridge, and Dublin universities did succeed in modernizing those institutions in ways that served middle-class interests. But the effect of this reorganization "made the universities more exclusive in terms of class than they had ever been. From 1854 to 1904 was the most difficult time for the poor scholar to make his way to Oxford and Cambridge."[8] This was achieved in part by opening up to competition certain scholarships traditionally available only to poor scholars, thereby assuring success for the better prepared sons of the middle class. The introduction of competitive examination, designed to open doors on the basis of merit, in fact worked against any student unable to prepare himself through costly schooling, as Hardy's Jude Fawley discovers. In the same way, public schools and even grammar schools which had had provisions for educating indigent local scholars, were suddenly closed to the lower classes.[9]

Within these upper-middle class educational institutions, despite some pressure for reform, the curricula continued to emphasize the classics. Although outdated in terms of the intellectual needs of the society, the classics had an important role to play. As historian Lawrence Stone notes, the latent function of a classical education by the seventeenth century was "the reservation of higher culture as the distinctive monopoly of a social elite."[10] He quotes from the Taunton Commission which reported to Parliament in 1868 on the endowed schools: "Professional men and lesser gentry 'value [the classics] highly for their own sake, and perhaps even more for the value at present assigned to them in English Society. They have nothing to look to but education to keep their sons on a high social level.'"[11] Study of the classics was consciously reserved for the sons of the upper-middle class in order to ensure their class status. The use of education to define and enforce class distinctions is evident in Robert Lowe's *Primary and Classical Education.* Writing in 1867, looking ahead to the provision for universal education which would come three years later, Lowe wrote that the lower classes should "be educated that they may appreciate and defer to a higher cultivation when they meet it; and the higher classes ought to be educated in a very different manner, in order that they may exhibit to the lower classes that higher education to which, if it were shown them, they would bow down and defer."[12] Lowe reminds us how palpably the culture of the upper-middle class was a tool which helped to maintain the hegemony of that class and how much access to that culture was deliberately withheld from other classes. Simon concludes his study of educational reforms by acknowledging that they helped to create

> a rationally organised system of secondary and higher education; one primarily designed for the benefit of the Victorian upper-middle class but which ensured the preservation of aristocratic privileges and pretensions while also opening new opportunities to professional men and the more prosperous tradesmen. [However,] the secondary school system had been remodelled to underline and reinforce class distinctions. In particular, the vast majority of working-class children were consciously debarred from receiving an education above their station. The handful who might in future succeed in making their way upwards would inevitably do so—and this was the intention—at the cost of alienation from their own class and local community.[13]

In short, as opportunities for upward mobility increased, and with it the tendency of the class structure to be fluid and open, this change was met with resistance. The upper-middle class, determined to defend its interests, maintained a throttlehold on the education system, using the touchstone of "culture" to legitimate its privileges and to debar the lower classes from sharing them.

During the last quarter of the nineteenth century, as the establishment consolidated its power, the working class emerged as a political and ideological opposition. The Second Reform Bill of 1867 included in the franchise some artisans and upper-working class men, although less than one-tenth of the population could vote. Nevertheless, this reform was perceived as a giant stride toward democracy—to some as a giant stride toward anarchy. The Education Act providing for universal primary schooling was passed in 1870, the secret ballot was accepted in 1872, and in 1884 the franchise was extended to another two million people. The Trades Union Congress was formed in 1871, the Social Democratic Federation in 1881, and the Independent Labour Party in 1893. By the end of the century the working class had emerged as a political and social presence, which did not share—and had systematically been prevented from sharing—the "culture" of the middle classes.

Nineteenth-century discourse about culture was discourse about class. In the last third of the century, the key contributor to the debate was Matthew Arnold, whose role was to erase the connection between the two terms, and simultaneously to reify and spiritualize culture as an inner quality divorced from material circumstances. Disenchanted with the social order created by the industrial and commerical middle classes, he argued that wealth had debased or "materialised" the entire society from the top down. The standard of culture which once had been represented by the aristocracy had been lost; the new society lacked the moral authority and legitimacy of the old caste system, as his perjorative labels suggest: Barbarians, Philistines, Populace. But Arnold was not simply a political reactionary, nor was a Tory-style return to the past possible. He was very close to Schiller and Goethe in his definition of culture as an inward ideal of wholeness, and he used the concept, as they had earlier, to criticize the fragmentation and rationalization of human beings required by an industrial society. To maintain this ideal while barring the door to "anarchy" (i.e., political democracy), Arnold called for a new definition of culture as an "*inward* condition of the mind and spirit." Culture was no longer to be "an engine of social and class distinction, separating its holder, like a badge or title, from other people who have not got it," but "a study of perfection . . . which consists in becoming something rather than in having something, in an inward condition of the mind and spirit, not in an outward set of circumstances. . . . a harmonious expansion of all the powers which make the beauty and worth of human nature."[14] Under the banner of culture he wanted to enroll "a certain number of aliens," men detached from any class, to be a saving "remnant" which would provide moral leadership in a society moving toward "anarchy."[15] The contradictions in his thought suggest his ambivalence about democracy: his purportedly classless ideal results in the creation of a new elite which will be the guardian of culture; and culture itself is conceived as a quintessentially human love of perfection, which is nevertheless possessed by only a select number of men.

Arnold's notion that culture could be thus disembodied was a dream. The notion of "unclassed aliens" serving as guardians of culture ignored the fact that culture played a crucial role in defining and legitimating class distinctions.[16] A cultivated manner precisely did separate, indeed was intended to separate, "its holder, like a badge or title, from other people," and cultivation was generally equated with the manners, tastes, and habits of the established middle class. Accent, dress, ease in social discourse, a certain level of decorum, familiarity with the classics—such outward signs of inner refinement were to a considerable extent acquired at school. A self-educated man or one trained in the local board schools and in the provincial colleges would not readily acquire the manner of an upper-middle class gentleman, and without it he was socially handicapped, whatever his abilities.

Arnold's definition of culture as an "inward condition of the mind and spirit," unrelated to class and therefore potentially available to all, might appeal both to a man within the established middle class who wanted to justify his superior social position and to a man below that class who wanted to justify his movement into it. Yet by divorcing an individual's inner development, his pursuit of culture, from his social position, Arnold made upward mobility problematic for the man whose main chance to develop himself depended on his moving into the bourgeoisie. In protesting that no class represented a degree of cultivation worthy of emulation, Arnold in effect stigmatized the upwardly mobile as a group moved by a spirit of commerical competition rather than by the love of cultural values associated with a higher class. His classless elite was a satisfactory notion if one already enjoyed the middle-class advantages of material security, a good education, and a promising career. But his spiritualized version of bourgeois individualism—the freedom to cultivate the self without respect to material or social estate—was in fact an unattainable ideal for those who might find it most appealing: the aspiring men from the culturally disenfranchised lower-middle and working classes. In this way Arnold directly contributed to their double bind.[17]

Class, Culture, and Double Bind: New Themes in the Bildungsroman

Of the four authors included in this study, Lawrence alone might be said to come from the working class, although his mother was petty bourgeois with decidedly middle-class aspirations for her sons. Gissing's father was a self-educated chemist, Hardy's an independent mason, Bennett's a potter who worked his way through night school to become a solicitor. All the sons were ambitious to move beyond the limited circumstances of their youth and to find a career which would develop their considerable talent. By their late twenties, all were determined to make their living by writing. Through their fiction they gained fame, income, and the opportunity to mix with a well-educated, upper-middle class society. This is true even of Gissing, who earned only a modest income from his writing and whose unfortunate marriages prevented him from moving much in society; nevertheless he counted among his friends distinguished men and women from the upper-middle class. Gissing excepted, their lives were outwardly success stories of upward mobility; inwardly all were "aliens," unclassed men who remained uncomfortably homeless, "wandering between two worlds," and their novels reflect this subjective reality.

In the childhood and youth of these writers, the conditions of life for their families were dangerously close to the proletarian world. All had kin who were laborers, among them men and women who had lost their economic independence and slipped into the abyss of indignity. These served as a warning that the possibility of sliding into the depths of the working class was real. Fifty years earlier neither Gissing, Hardy, Bennett nor Lawrence could have hoped for a financially secure, middle-class career as writers; all benefited from the political and educational reforms and from the new opportunities for mobility. By good fortune and with family support, they enjoyed that margin of freedom from immediate economic want and a measure of schooling which made upward mobility possible. Their aspirations, their material opportunities, and their dread of the insecure and limited world of the working class were typical of the petty bourgeois who, in the new economic and social order, *had* to move up or risk sinking into a lower class.

However, upward mobility involved a psychological double bind for these men; success inspired feelings of betrayal and estrangement. Their individual achievement had been fostered by the hopes, the encouragement, and the sacrifices of families which they had left behind in rising. Their repugnance for the narrowness of the world they had escaped was accompanied by a sense of guilt about their own good fortune and a sense of ongoing connection with a world they had intended to leave behind. Moreover, their acceptance into the middle class was hard-won; the establishment greeted these unclassed authors with interest and even enthusiasm while eyeing with condescension any lapse from its own standard of cultivation. While all made close friends among the upper-middle class, none found a community which assuaged his sense of being an outsider.

Further, these authors saw their own mobility as part of the great social transformation of their time; the very conditions which permitted their rise were, they believed, destroying that level of culture which in the past had given value to social ascendance. To varying degrees these writers felt compromised by their participation in what Hardy called "the modern vice of unrest." "Bounders," men of low standards, esthetically and morally, bourgeois individualists whose motive was self-aggrandizement rather than self-development—these were the upwardly mobile. "To have a good chance of being one of his country's worthies [a man] should be as cold-blooded as a fish and as selfish as a pig," Hardy observes in *Jude the Obscure*. But at the same time *not* to move up, *not* to escape the material limitations of a petty-bourgeois environment, *not* to find a way to cultivate one's intellect and sensibility—this too amounted to betrayal of one's potential. In either rising or failing to rise, the individual was compromised.

In *Born in Exile, Jude the Obscure, Clayhanger, Sons and Lovers,* and *The Rainbow,* these authors use the Bildungsroman to record their subjective experience of upward mobility. Their protagonists, partially self-portraits, are provincial, lower-middle or working-class youths who aspire to develop themselves. They are distinguished from others around them by their ambition, intelligence, and sensibility. As Hardy wrote of Jude, each is "a species of Dick Whittington whose spirit [is] touched to finer issues than a mere material gain." All are would-be writers or artists who fail to realize their full potential. The authors explore the psychology of these youths: their passivity and lack of confidence, coupled with pride, ambition, and a strong sense of their superiority or individuality; their shame and anger which can turn inward into self-contempt; their intense self-consciousness, unrelieved by constructive activity; their consciousness of mingled resentment, envy, and contempt for the classes above and below them.

Each of the protagonists is a young Arnoldian, consciously pursuing an ideal of self-cultivation in true Bildungsroman-style. He conceives of culture as an "inward condition" and thinks that his moral and intellectual growth is (or should be) unrelated to his economic and social situation. In some cases he is further alienated from family members who have merely material ambitions for him. Naively, egoistically, romantically, he believes that the particular quality of his ambition connects him with a classless elite which exists somewhere beyond his own narrow community and which will eventually recognize him as a member of their select, superior group. The naiveté of this conviction is exposed in the author's ironic treatment of his protagonist.

In pursuing his spiritualized ideal of self-cultivation, the protagonist encounters material obstacles: limited opportunities for education; a precarious economic situation which obliges him to take up unsatisfying work at an early age; contemptuous rejection by people with power and prestige. These material disadvantages are of course very much related to class, and unless he can overcome them, his progress must be radically limited. To develop fully, he must be able to move at ease in a cultivated world which lies beyond his present horizon and to draw on its resources with confidence. To do this, he must belie his origins and cultivate the manner of the establishment. He must pursue his ambition covertly, without appearing to be a social climber. Eventually he discovers that what he had projected as an ideally cultivated world is in itself unworthy, intellectually compromised, snobbish, petty, exclusive, and in its own way narrow. This paradigm is most closely realized in *Born in Exile* where Gissing boldly imagines the full extent of self-betrayal and loss of integrity required for his protagonist to insinuate himself into the upper-middle class. I argue that the other three writers share Gissing's anxiety: he has proposed the dilemma from which their characters shrink in uncertainty and confusion.

While there are always external obstacles to self-development, in each novel the protagonist's failure is also related to inner weaknesses which appear to be character flaws. Jude Fawley, Godwin Peak, Paul Morel, and Edwin Clayhanger all are filled with a mixture of pride and self-doubt that is difficult to judge; we wonder how much potential they really have and whether they are deluded about their abilities. They are hesitant and indecisive, dreamers rather than doers, "sensitive plants" not well suited to struggle. However, in exploring the situation of the unclassed man, the authors help us to recognize how thoroughly his diffidence is related to his social situation. We learn we have to erase the distinction between external and internal factors and see that society and the psyche have combined to limit his development. His self-doubt is not idiosyncratic weakness but the representative response of a talented and sensitive member of the petty bourgeoisie.

For the unclassed man all avenues towards harmonious and integrated self-development are effectively closed. Movement up is a fradulent, self-compromising process. Even the wish for upward mobility is associated with fear of failure, guilt, loss, and estrangement from any class. His economic situation is sufficiently precarious to preclude his retreat into a private world in which he might develop inwardly apart from society. He cannot cultivate himself by embracing the narrow world beneath him, as Pip does, for these authors know the working world too well to be sentimental about its inadequacies. The ideal solution to his predicament, membership in a classless elite, proves in each case to be an unattainable dream.

Writing about Gissing, V. S. Pritchett observed that while "the great Russian novels of the nineteenth century arose from the failure of a class . . . the English sprang out of its success."[18] The writers included in this study belonged to a class which lacked confidence, which was fearful of failure and anxious about success, and which could neither celebrate wholeheartedly the triumph of bourgeois individualism nor accept the alternative of class solidarity. They speak for people caught in the middle, who experienced the breakdown of liberal ideology as an anxious, guilt-ridden personal crisis. In choosing to reflect upon their experience in the ideologically freighted Bildungsroman, these writers make the genre itself a site of conflict. Their novels register the distance between the promises of the Bildungsroman and the social experience they had to record, exposing the gap between ideology and history.

A Note on Method

I assume that literature reflects and refers to, comments on and changes social experience, and that it is one of the tasks of criticism to explore this connection between art and society. In one sense this is not a problematical matter with the novels in hand, since in them the authors draw extensively upon the experiences of their young manhood; the content indubitably alludes to specific historical circumstances. However, the interesting questions concern what the authors thought about their experience, and here we enter the realm of ideology, of how they imagined their relationship to a given social reality.[19]

By "ideology" I mean not "false consciousness" but that inescapable social consciousness, that picture of the world which every person must acquire as he or she grows up in a particular society at a particular time. That there will be competing pictures of the world is also true, and I assume that in the nineteenth century, class is the major determinant of competing ideologies. One's experience necessarily will be understood within the context of ideology, and it is the task of ideology to smooth over contradictions, to present experience as orderly and natural. But contradictions cannot be entirely repressed; they demand our attention and show up in literary texts as writers worry over and attempt to resolve them imaginatively. They may show up, too, as absences or silences about that which text cannot bear to become aware, or in disorder and stylistic disjunctions through which the "political unconscious" presses to make itself known.

By the end of the nineteenth century, the bourgeois ideology of individualism was in acute crisis, and particularly so for the authors included in this study. Certain contradictions emerged with particular force: the sheer psychological pressure to compete was uncomfortably intense, and the world created by that competition was in many ways repugnant; because the individual felt he had no choice in the matter of rising, the self he "made" through that effort seemed alien and often deformed; and the obstacles to his rise, both internal and external, made the notion that the individual was free to shape his destiny highly dubious. In choosing the Bildungsroman form, the authors indicate that they continue to see their stories as individual histories, but in the process of telling their stories, they expose contradictions which belie that assumption—sometimes through conscious protest, sometimes indirectly through irony or dialogic narration, sometimes simply in the act of representing that experience against the ideological assumptions of the genre. That the contradictions are not understood as effects of a particular social organization but as personal failure and psychological breakup, is evidenced in the authors' uncertain distance from their characters. With Lawrence and

Hardy in particular the crisis in liberal ideology pressed them to break the realistic and organic forms of the Bildungsroman and to move toward metaphysic and myth as ways of explaining their protagonists' situation. I have sought to account for formal innovation and disjunction within the novels in terms of ideological conflict, seeing the genre itself as a bearer of ideology.

I see my work as a part of the ongoing resistance to thinking about literature as a self-referential system instead of exploring its connection to all those social practices through which we constitute our world. My approach has been influenced by the theoretical work of Georg Lukács, Lucien Goldmann, Raymond Williams, Terry Eagleton, and Fredric Jameson, and by other critics of the novel who have put that theory into practice: in particular, John Goode, Michael Holderness, Judith Lowder Newton, Mary Poovey, Scott Sanders, and Peter Smith.

Figure 1.   George Gissing, 1895
(By Permission of the British Library)

1

Gissing: The Unclassed Man

Gissing's reputation was initially as an English practitioner of French naturalism, a follower of the school of Zola and thus a student of the miseries of the lower classes. More recently, scholars have pointed out that his purportedly objective stance is colored by a profoundly conservative ideology. He had grown up in a society in which traditional distinctions of caste were dissolving in the newly forming class structure. While Gissing potentially stood to benefit from this new fluidity, he loathed the commercialization and democratization which accompanied the transformation. Profoundly distrustful of the fundamental Victorian faith in progress and the perfectibility of man, he opposed most of the social changes which swept England after 1870; in particular, he believed that mass education was one of the greatest threats to culture. Like Miniver Cheevy, he "cursed the commonplace" and yearned for the graces of the past. Unlike Cheevy, he was fascinated by the processes that were undoing the social order he so admired.

At the base of Gissing's fictional world are the working people of London: ignoble, depraved, ignorant beyond the help of education and, with rare exceptions, beyond redemption. Above this "nether world," and often catering to its passions, is the burgeoning commercial class, producing and peddling wares which reflect its own vulgarity and appeal to that of others. The only chance of insuring social order and preserving culture against the twin evils of democracy and philistinism is to maintain the power and prestige of an established upper-middle class. Change, especially social mobility, upsets the natural hierarchy of classes and threatens the elite which alone can preserve the values on which civilization depends.

Within this otherwise fixed world in which class determines character and destiny are the "unclassed" men and women who generate Gissing's plots. For the most part they are educated proletarians or petty bourgeois who seek their fortune and/or their identity by moving among the several classes. Whether they are schemers or idealists, their search raises doubts about the stability and legitimacy of the social hierarchy and introduces the possibility of change into the novels. However, the experiences of these unclassed characters confirm the reactionary view that the social hierarchy reflects genuine distinctions of intellect and sensibility and that social mobility threatens an established order which should be maintained.

In the early novels (*The Unclassed,* 1884; *Thyrza,* 1887; *The Nether World,* 1889) the philanthropic projects of the unclassed men, who hope to raise a submerged class through educational or social reform, prove futile. This futility is raised to a tragic intensity in *Thyrza* when the idealistic reformer Egremont destroys the happiness of those very working-class people he had sought to help. In *Demos* (1886) the proletarian Richard Mutimer is unclassed by an unexpected inheritance. Blind to his own coarseness and deluded by his egalitarian ideology, Mutimer denies that there are distinctions among classes. He puts his socialist ideals into practice by establishing an Owenite factory in the idyllic Wanley Valley and marries a well-bred, refined woman. But in the end Mutimer's inheritance proves to be a mistake, and his fortune is restored to a member of the local gentry. Wanley Valley is spared the blight of industry, and Mutimer meets his death at the hands of a mob, a victim of his illusions about "demos" and about himself. Gissing's idealized upper-middle class has virtually disappeared in the commercial world of *New Grub Street* (1891), where the increased possibility for social mobility is associated with the rapid deterioration of culture. In *Born in Exile* (1892) a baseborn man who attempts to ally himself with the gentry is discovered to be a *poseur* and is expelled for his presumption. With few exceptions (such as Ida Starr and Waymark in *The Unclassed*), the people who attempt to cross class lines wreck their lives; the divisions between the classes are consistently maintained and implicitly affirmed at the close of each novel.

At least two critics, Alan Swingewood and Fredric Jameson, have argued that Gissing's early novels are experiments (in the Zola-ean sense) designed to prove the inalterability of the class structure. But as Jameson points out, there is considerably more to Gissing than this. More than any other writer in English, Gissing makes us aware of the intolerable strain of the existing class structure. Again and again his characters transgress class boundaries only to bring misery on themselves and others, but their defeat and the sheer burden of class consciousness registered in these novels have, Jameson argues, "a more radicalizing effect, in spite of the reactionary reflexions with which [they are] accompanied, than the sentimental and condescending working-class novels of the period or the mere satirico-ethical denunciation of the corruption and immorality of bourgeois or aristocratic high life."[1] With profound psychological insight in an area quite ignored by other writers, Gissing explores the resentment and envy which accompany class-consciousness. His awareness had been finely tuned by his own experiences in unclassing, and his penetrating psychological studies of his characters derive, I argue, from self-analysis.

Nowhere is his anatomy of class-consciousness more penetrating and more complete than in his semi-autobiographical Bildungsroman, *Born in Exile,* in which he charts the development of and the contradictions involved in his own reactionary stance.

*   *   *

George Gissing (1857–1903) was born in Wakefield, Yorkshire, the oldest son of a lower-middle-class chemist. An intelligent, disciplined student, he was expected to climb the narrow educational ladder; at fourteen he won a scholarship to Owens College, Manchester, where he took many prizes and passed the matriculation examination for the University of London. Aiming at a distinguished career as a classicist, Gissing planned to go up in the fall of 1876. While still at Owens, straining his talent and resources to join a cultivated elite, Gissing became involved with a young prostitute and, acting as her benefactor, stole from his fellow students to support her. His expulsion from the college permanently closed a virtually assured entrée into the upper-middle class. His relationship with the girl and, even more, the crime itself suggest that Gissing felt psychologically alienated from the social group which he idealized and to which he aspired to belong. Whatever his motives, the trauma surrounding the incident contributed to Gissing's sense of permanent unfitness for middle-class society.[2]

After a brief period in prison and a trip to America, Gissing returned to England, lived in the London slums, and began *Workers in the Dawn* (1880) about a youth of artistic sensibility whose conscience leads him to undertake social reform for the urban poor among whom he was reared. Yet this sympathy for the despised and downtrodden—the sort of sympathy which probably contributed to his crime at Owens—did not make Gissing an advocate of liberal reform. Class mattered too much to Gissing to allow him to credit a democratic vision of social harmony among equals. Already in his second novel, *The Unclassed* (1884) Gissing was analyzing the complex motives which could inform youthful radicalism. His autobiographical character Waymark reflects:

> I was not a conscious hypocrite in those days of violent radicalism, working-man's club lecturing, and the like; the fault was that I understood myself as yet so imperfectly. That zeal on behalf of the suffering masses was nothing more nor less than disguised zeal on behalf of my own starved passions.... I identified myself with the poor and ignorant; I did not make their cause my own, but my own cause theirs.[3]

From early on Gissing recognized that resentment or envy could inform political allegiances. In this novel and later in *Thyrza* (1887) he questioned this misguided negative identification of an idealistic youth with the working class, and in *Demos* (1886) he explored the dubious motives of the proletarian Richard Mutimer. After his own youthful identification with the oppressed, Gissing seems to have felt alienated both from the class he had sought to help and from the class he had hoped to enter. Social mobility, either upward or downward, had proved impossible psychologically, and this deadlock found expression in his stories of unclassed men who are unable, whatever their motives, to cross class lines. Although in his last years he achieved a measure of fame and financial security, he remained a perpetual outsider.

In *Born in Exile* (1892) Gissing explored the stress involved in the experience of unclassing, drawing extensively on his own background in the creation of his protagonist Godwin Peak, an aggressively independent youth bent on rising by his own merits from the shop-keeping class he despises. "Peak is myself—one phase of myself," Gissing wrote a friend, adding, "It is a novel I had to write."[4] He probes Peak's anxieties about his identity, his fierce sense of superiority combined with powerful feelings of inadequacy and unworthiness, his contradictory desire to belong to what he despises. The novel depicts with great subtlety Peak's psychological development toward the crucial moment of self-betrayal and the painful rendering of social situations in which Peak finds it quite impossible to "be himself." *Born in Exile* offers the clearest paradigm of the double bind faced by the upwardly mobile petty bourgeois who can develop himself only by rising but whose rising requires him to compromise his integrity.

*   *   *

At the opening of the novel, Peak is a promising scholarship student at a provincial college in the mid-1870s. Named for the radical philosopher, Godwin Peak is an aggressive individualist, a freethinker and rationalist who considers himself "an aristocrat of nature's own making—one of the few highly favoured beings who, in despite of circumstance, are pinnacled above mankind" (41). Arrogant and egocentric, he is also acutely self-conscious about his poverty, and though he maintains a haughty bearing toward the other students, he is ashamed and defensive about his own and his family's lack of "breeding." Book One is an insightful study of how social and intellectual insecurities cooperate to drive Peak from the college before he has taken his degree.

Ten years pass before we next see Godwin, frustrated by his work in an obscure chemical manufacturing plant and by his inability to find an appropriate avenue for his talent and ambition. His contempt for the "vulgar poor" of London, among whom he has been forced to live, has turned him into a scornful anti-democrat who argues that a rigid class structure alone can preserve culture—that culture from which he is still largely excluded, that culture which is rooted in the Christian tradition which Peak, as a freethinker, despises intellectually. His envy and resentment of the well-to-do, which are so much a part of Peak's psychology in Book One, take a new, unconscious shape as he considers a possible way of entering the upper-middle class. "I have no other ambition in life . . . my one supreme desire is to marry a perfectly refined woman. Put it in the correct terms: I am a plebian, and I aim at marrying a lady" (140). However, he despairs of ever realizing this ambition.

A chance encounter with an old school friend gives Peak his opportunity. He visits the Warricombes at their country house and pretends to be a theological student. This role, adopted on a momentary impulse, is so effective that Peak determines to play the conscious hypocrite and actually to enter the Church, a career he abhors intellectually but which is profoundly in harmony with his social convictions. He maintains his entrée with the Warricombes and eventually wins the love of their beautiful, devout daughter; unmasked at the moment of his declaration, Peak is hounded out of England to die as he was born—in exile from the only society which, he feels, could have nurtured his sensibility and talent.

We close the novel uncertain how to judge Peak. Is he a talented man driven by society to desperate stratagems, or a repulsive interloper, a flunkey who proves that, irrespective of brains, birth and class tell? Does his fate affirm the stability of the social hierarchy or suggest that something is desperately wrong with the class structure? Preserving a coldly neutral, detached tone in analyzing Peak, the narrator refuses to guide our judgment.

In Peak, Gissing combined antithetical character types which he had used before in his fiction: the crass materialist on the make and the alienated intellectual, illustrated by such pairs as Milvain and Reardon in *New Grub Street* or Mutimer and Eldon in *Demos*. Heretofore Gissing had scrupulously separated two kinds of ambition. The Mutimers and Milvains are demagogues, attracted to the urban jungle and willing to compromise themselves for material gain. The Eldons and Reardons hold to their ideals before the rising tide of vulgar materialism and maintain their integrity in the face of crushing poverty. Excluded from the upper-middle class, they nevertheless share its values and have a profound, almost effete horror of "the people." Peak combines the pride, the sensibility, and the conservative values of the latter type with the lack of integrity of a Milvain or Mutimer.

In combining the passive but worthy idealist and the successful but corrupt materialist, Gissing communicated his sense of the dilemma faced by any educated lower-class youth in the closing decades of the nineteenth century. In order to become one of the simple, integrated, refined souls who embody his aristocratic ideal, Peak must pretend to be what he is not. He cannot succeed without such pretense, and yet it is de facto evidence of his unworthiness. This double bind at the core of the novel—the impossibility of succeeding in the project of upward mobility—seems to confirm the reactionary view that the social structure is unalterable, and even desirably so, since thereby the integrity of the establishment is maintained. But the double bind also renders absurd this inalterability and delegitimizes the ideal of integrity by involving us in Peak's no-win situation.

In order better to grasp Peak's peculiar situation and character, it may help to view him in terms of a distinction Lionel Trilling develops in *Sincerity and Authenticity*. Drawing on Hegel's *Phenomenology of Spirit*, Trilling distinguishes between two kinds of selfhood: that of the "honest soul" and that of the "base self," characterized by a "disintegrated consciousness." The honest soul, a noble, cultivated figure, moves in a world of "affluent decorum . . . of order, peace, honour, and beauty, these qualities being realized in, and dependent upon, certain material conditions."[5] What Trilling calls a "bourgeoisified" version of this ideal is embodied in *Born in Exile* in the Warricombe family, in whose home Peak carries out his deception. Peak is drawn to the Warricombes' "large and joyous scheme of life. . . . Merely to step upon the carpet fluttered his senses: merely to breathe the air was a purification. Luxury of the rational kind, dictated by regard for health of body and soul, appeared in every detail" (167). Such a setting nurtures the noble, cultivated man, whom Hegel describes as the "honest soul." This honest soul exists "in a wholly harmonious relation to the external power of society, to the point of being identified with it. . . . In its consciousness there is no division, it is at one with itself. It is not shaped by its beneficent intentions towards others; its intention is wholly towards itself." This noble ideal of self-cultivation and integrity, with centuries of tradition behind it, dominates Peak's imagination.

In contrast to the honest soul, the base self is a man of low station who becomes conscious that he resents a wealth and power structure which denies him material advantages. The base self rejects the noble or honest soul's "wholly harmonious relation" to the external order and begins to carry out "self-serving" purposes "beyond the limits deemed appropriate to its social status. These purposes can be realized only by covert means and are therefore shameful. Between the intentions of the base self and its avowals there is no congruence." The base self may pay lip service to the power structure while seeking its own ends, a stage of revolt which Hegel terms "the heroism of flattery." The loss of integrity continues:

> In refusing its obedient service to the state power and to wealth [the base self] has lost its wholeness; its selfhood is "disintegrated"; the self is "alienated" from itself. But because it has detached itself from imposed conditions, Hegel says that it has made a step in progress. He puts it that the existence of the self "on its own account is, strictly speaking, the loss of itself." The statement can also be made the other way round: "Alienation of self is really self-preservation."

Hegel's description of the development of the base self through alienation and disintegration provides a paradigm for Peak. Like the base self, he aspires to be noble, but his activity can only alienate him from his ideal. Despite his own and his author's professed admiration for the honest soul, his "disintegrated consciousness" claims our attention as a more strenuous (or authentic) mode of being. In conflict here are not only two conceptions of the self but two conceptions of culture. On the one hand Matthew Arnold writes of "the development of the self to perfection through its active experience of 'the best that is thought and said in the world,'" an idea of culture which depends upon the world of affluent decorum. On the other hand Hegel defines Bildung as "the characteristic field of experience of the base self; it proposes the activity by which the disintegrated, alienated, and distraught consciousness expresses its negative relation with the external power of society and thereby becomes 'Spirit truly objective,' that is, self-determining." In seeking to enter the Warricombes' world by devious means, Peak expresses his "negative relation with the external power of society." Gissing is far from intending to undermine the ideal of affluent decorum; he expects us to criticize Peak's base envy and hypocrisy. Yet the only moral vantage point from which we may criticize is that of the honest soul, which by the end of the novel has been exposed in its simplicity by a "disintegrated consciousness" which dominates our imagination not because of what it believes but because of what it has dared to violate. The Hegelian conception of self-culture prompts us to consider that the possibilities for spiritual growth may lie not in the country house from which Peak is excluded but in the disintegrative process which he undergoes.

*   *   *

Peak's peculiarly intense self-consciousness and the combination of scorn, envy, and admiration that he feels for the honest souls of the Warricombe family claim our interest and make him something more than a flunkey. His conception of himself—of what he could be and what he is—is at once stimulated and distorted by the class structure. His aggressive individualism, his idealism, and his snobbery are inextricably intertwined. Gissing's forte lies in showing the extent to which Peak's self-consciousness is generated by his class-consciousness.

Peak is "no common lad"; he is unquestionably intelligent, curious, and self-disciplined as well as egotistical and arrogant. His initial integrity is pointedly confirmed in an otherwise inconsequential anecdote about the boy's conscientious behavior when given the chance to cheat on a test. As a promising scholar, his ambition is superior "to all thought of material gain," and he rejects his family's bribe to send him to college if he will become a "parson."

> A youth whose brain glowed like a furnace, whose heart throbbed with tumult of high
> ambitions, of inchoate desires; endowed with knowledge altogether exceptional for his years;
> a nature essentially militant, displaying itself in innumerable forms of callow
> intolerance.... What is to be done with the boy?
>
> All very well, if the question signified, in what way to provide for the healthy development
> of his manhood. Of course it meant nothing of the sort, but merely: What work can be found
> for him whereby he may earn his daily bread? We—his kinsfolk even, not to think of the
> world at large—can have no concern with his growth as an intellectual being. (38-39)

Although in general Gissing is coldly analytical in his treatment of Peak, the foregoing passage betrays considerable empathy with the petty-bourgeois boy caught up in the Arnoldian dream of belonging to an unclassed cultural elite and thus alienated from the mundane concerns of his family.

Talent, "high ambitions," and a sensibility that is rubbed raw by a cockney accent encourage Peak to think of himself as "born in exile." Material circumstances belie his inner nobility, and the effort to realize that nobility brings him into conflict with an external order which limits his development. From earliest youth his "strongest emotions seem to be absorbed in revolt" (404), and in maturity he reflects: "Born a rebel, how could his be the fate of those happy men who are at one with the order of things?" (248) His intellect has been shaped by this spirit of opposition; as a child "already it was the habit of his mind to associate popular dogma with intellectual shallowness; herein, as at every other point which fell within his scope, he had begun to scorn average people, and to pride himself intensely on views which he found generally condemned" (37). His ambition is fired by contempt for his peers: "There's nothing I hate like vulgarity. That's why I can't stand Roper.... I'm working like a nigger at algebra and Euclid this half, just because I think it would almost kill me to be beaten ... by a low cad" (41). And when his brother buys a faddish hat, he erupts:

> "Can't you feel ... that it's a disgrace to buy and wear such a thing? ... anyone who respects
> himself should choose something as different as possible.... It's bad enough to follow when
> you can't help it, but to imitate asses gratuitously is the lowest depth of degradation. Don't
> you know that that is the meaning of vulgarity? ... Have you no *self*? Are you made, like this
> hat, on a pattern with a hundred thousand others?" (76)

Peak's snobbery is part of his desperate attempt to distance himself from his material and social circumstances, to create another identity. The honest soul in harmony with the established order need not struggle to be and therefore does not know itself and is not self-aware. Peak's more demanding notion of a "self" that is made, not born, is a step toward that freedom from matter which Hegel hoped the base self would eventually attain. Peak's sense of this "self" depends upon his conscious effort to alienate himself from his petty-bourgeois background. Struggling against material circumstances to bring his noble soul into being, Peak cannot easily be true to himself; he rejects what he is to keep faith with what he may become.

From the outset of his career, Peak is obliged to maintain an "elaborate hypocrisy" with his family and to assume "a false position" with his patrons, the Whitelaws, whose money is his "servitude." "Am I to be grateful for a mere chance of earning my living? Have I not shown that I am capable of something more than the ordinary lot in life?" Peak protests (95). The quality of his ambition is lost on family and friends who hope only that something "advantageous" may come his way. The very word drives Peak into a frenzy of shame, for it betrays the self-seeking attitude of the base self which he, the aristocrat-in-exile, would avoid at all cost. He resents the efforts of others to further his career, for their acts make him feel his dependence. When the founder of the college offers Peak a scholarship, he at first accepts it as an act of

> Medicean patronage. For the moment no faintest doubt gave warning to his self-respect; he was eager to accept nobly a benefaction nobly intended. Later he felt his dependence in a way he had not foreseen; the very clothes he wore, fresh from the tailor's, seemed to be the gift of charity, and their stiffness shamed him. (45, 47)

When high social rank and its attendant wealth and power were matters solely of birth rather than of personal worth, patronage could be conferred on talented men without implying a lack of respect. But Peak's feelings of baseness and resentment are inevitable in a capitalist society come to power on an ideology of individualism with a commitment to rising by merit; in such a society patronage becomes a shaming gesture.

Peak's material circumstances simply do not permit him to behave in a way which is consonant with his image of himself. He must quash his self-respect and pride and pretend gratitude when he feels resentment; before Lady Whitelaw he feels that "his position was a false one: to be begging with awkward show of thankfulness for a benefaction which in his heart he detested. He knew himself for an undesigning hypocrite, and felt that he might as well have been a rascal complete" (95). Peak's identification with the honest soul and with the aristocratic world fosters a sense of self-division so powerful that ten years later his gross act of hypocrisy seems but the continuation of a duplicity which has dogged him all his life.

"With the growth of his militant egoism, there had developed in Godwin Peak an excess of nervous sensibility which threatened to deprive his character of the initiative rightly belonging to it" (54). This "sensibility" stems from his class-consciousness and makes Peak acutely aware of his own uncouthness and constantly fearful that his base origins will be disclosed in some small action. With students and teachers at Whitelaw College, Peak is equally unable to "be himself," for he is both shamed by and bitterly envious of their "gentility" and "delicate culture." He withdraws into a sullen aloofness to protect his self-esteem, despising "those of his fellow-students who had the social air.... Yet did it chance that one of these offensive youths addressed a civil word to him, on the instant his prejudice was disarmed, and his emotions flowed forth in a response to which he would gladly have given free expression" (51). Though moved by their graciousness, Peak is unable to express his admiration or gratitude; his inability to be anything other than "boorish" shames him the more. That "nervous sensibility" which is but the other side of his aggressive assertion of his superiority proves his downfall when his uncle decides to open "Peak's Dinin' and Refreshment Rooms" across from the gates of the college. Peak cannot bear this reminder of his ignoble origins, and he leaves school without taking his degree.

For the most part Gissing confines himself to a neutral presentation of Peak's state of mind, abjuring either sympathy or contempt. His character is unattractive, but Gissing well understands the forces that have (mis) shaped him. In the following passage Gissing explains the dilemma of any intelligent man who has to *act* the gentleman.

> The play of the imaginative and speculative faculties accounts for the common awkwardness of intelligent young men in society that is strange to them. Only the cultivation of a *double consciousness* puts them finally at ease. Impossible to converse with suavity, and to heed the forms of ordinary good-breeding, when the brain is absorbed in all manner of new problems: one must learn *to act a part,* to control the facial mechanism, to observe and anticipate, even whilst the intellect is spending its sincere energy on subjects unavowed. (71, emphasis added)

The honest soul, as we know, does not experience such self-division. Gissing continues:

> The perfectly graceful man will always be he who has no strong apprehension either of his own personality or of that of others, who lives on the surface of things, who can be interested without emotion, and surprised without contemplative impulse.

Because he has no need to struggle, the honest soul develops his "self" less; the moral effort involved in being what he is, in being "true" to himself, is not strenuous. The paragraph concludes with Peak's recognition that his intense self-consciousness contributes to his problems:

> Never yet had Godwin Peak uttered a word that was worth listening to, or made a remark that declared his mental powers, save in most familiar colloquy. He was beginning to understand the various reasons of his seeming clownishness, but this very process of self-study opposed an obstacle to improvement.

Gissing acknowledges dispassionately that Peak's project of becoming an honest soul is doomed to failure without a hint of irony about the vacuity of the "perfectly graceful man," without any suggestion that the "improvement" Peak desires is a questionable ideal, and without any intimation that such "double consciousness" will be morally compromising. The passage is an instance of what Fredric Jameson calls "blank irony," which comes into play when Gissing preserves a deadening neutrality in presenting characters whose thoughts are charged with class-consciousness; the "blankness" of the irony alerts us to the author's unresolved problem of judging his character.[6]

* * *

The hyper-self-consciousness and sense of duplicity which Peak feels throughout his youth prepare us for his dissimulation in Book Two. His ten-year sojourn in London has taught him how long "nature's aristocrat" may be ignored by society. Intellectually he has matured into a bitter rationalist at war with convention, scorning the popular attempts to reconcile science and religion in order to preserve the old morality—and the old hierarchy. His own literary effort, a savagely satirical article entitled "The New Sophistry," is directed against such intellectual compromises. But temperamentally Peak is more conservative than ever, supporting "a true distinction of social classes" based on birth as a way of preserving society from the coarseness and vulgarity of the people. "The masses are not only fools, but very near brutes. Yes, they can send forth fine individuals—but remain base. . . . the lower classes are always disagreeable, often repulsive, sometimes hateful" (134), Peak tells his friend Earwaker, who wonders silently how Peak reconciles such a view with his own social origins. Are we to accept this as Peak's unconscious judgment of himself—a fine individual who remains base? Cursed with a "modern temper," Peak's intellectual convictions and conservative sensibility pull him in opposite directions. "Sincerity" would condemn him to continuing self-division in a world in which "only the worse elements of his character [would find] nourishment and range" (170).

Peak acknowledges that he is "a plebian" who aims at "marrying a lady." Unlike the socialist Richard Mutimer, he does not want to blur class distinctions by marrying above his rank. He is seeking a match for his inner nobility, a means of achieving that harmonious relation with the external order which will allow him to cultivate himself to the fullest. He is drawn to Sidwell Warricombe because she lives in a world of wholeness and beauty which appeals to his own disharmony. In pursing the ideal of the honest soul he hopes to shed his spirit of revolt, his "ignoble self-consciousness," his alienation. His masquerade is conducted to find an identity, an integrity. He betrays himself in order to become himself.

However, Peak's attempt to *act* like an honest soul inevitably leads not to integrity but to pretense, to further alienation and to an even more intense, chaotic self-consciousness in which he is unable to locate any consistent "self" at all. By dissimulating, he plays the shameful part of the base self "between whose avowals and intentions there is no congruence"; like the base self, in usurping the place of the honest soul, Peak drags the whole ideal of nobility down about him. For instance, although he must compromise his intellectual convictions as a means to his goal, Peak rationalizes that the old religious dogmas have contributed to the stability of the social order. He tells Earwaker: "Depend upon it . . . There's a vast police force in them, at all events. A man may very strongly defend himself for preaching them" (136). He does not see that in lending his superior brain to prop up the religious foundation of a dying class structure, he is in fact undermining its legitimacy. Peak's attempt to imitate the upper-middle class in order to be accepted by it turns into an unconscious parody which exposes the moral and intellectual bankruptcy of his ideal. His imitation conceals his aggression against the external power relations which have denied him opportunities to develop.

Of course Peak's hostility is largely repressed, and his deception begins more or less by chance. When he first reveals to Earwaker his ambition to marry a lady, we hear contradictory voices within his "disintegrated consciousness" as Peak moves abruptly from a heated discussion of his rationalist views to his advocacy of a social hierarchy propped up by religious dogma. Shortly thereafter, he starts off on a holiday, planning to emigrate to Australia, but in Exeter he meets an old schoolmate, Buckland Warricombe, who invites him to lunch. Peak is overwhelmed by the opportunity to enjoy, even for a few hours, a level of material comfort and cultivation which he had long felt to be his proper estate. For the whole day he plays a part, unable to disentangle his "self" from the "actor."[7]

In the following passage we see how the "double consciousness" which Gissing described earlier still dogs Peak; even as he establishes in his own mind his credentials as a gentleman, Peak's ignobility is confirmed by his concluding perception that he may be able to use the Warricombes.

> No less introspective than in the old days, though he could better command his muscles, Peak, after each of his short remarks, made comparison of his tone and phraseology with those of the other speakers. Had he still any marks of the ignoble world from which he sprang? Any defect of pronunciation, any native awkwardness of utterance? . . . Buckland Warricombe was rather a careless talker, but it was the carelessness of a man who had never needed to reflect on such a matter, the refinement of whose enunciation was assured to him from the nursery. That now was a thing to be aimed at. . . . Heaven be thanked that he was unconcerned on the point of garb! . . . he defied inspection. Not Sidwell herself . . . could conceive a prejudice against him on this account. . . . Surely he could make good his claim to be deemed a gentleman. . . . Grant him a little time, and why should he not become a recognised friend of this family? If he were but resident in Exeter. (155–56)

Peak's "act" begins with this self-consciousness about appearing a gentleman, and his further pretense commences almost unconsciously when Sidwell catches him off guard asking if he has seen the cathedral. Peak volunteers that he has attended services there, an answer which is factually true but misleading. "Had he reflected, perhaps he would not have [so responded]; even in speaking he suffered a confused doubtfulness. But as soon as the words were uttered, he felt strangely glad" (156). Then, "under the marvelling regard of his conscious self," he finds he is able to speak cogently about a sermon to which he had scarcely listened and impress the family with the caliber of his mind turned to orthodox interests. "A new spirit...had strange possession of him.... By the oddest of intellectual processes he had placed himself altogether outside the sphere of unorthodox spirits" (159).

By acting Peak feels that he has called forth a new self, wholly in harmony with his surroundings. In the afternoon the Warricombes drive him to a prospect, and Peak feels so entirely a part of the group that he is able to enter into "the joyous tone of the occasion," and even to be "spontaneous" in conversation. As much as any of the Warricombes, Peak fully responds to the "rural loveliness," a sure sign of the genuinely cultivated soul in a Gissing novel. From across the valley they view the seat of Sir Stafford Northcote.

> The house had no architectural beauty, but its solitary lordship...declared the graces and privileges of ancestral wealth. Standing here alone, Godwin would have surveyed these possessions of an English aristocrat with more or less bitterness; envy would...have perturbed his pleasure in the natural scene. Accompanied as he was...he exulted in the prerogatives of birth and opulence, felt proud of hereditary pride, gloried that his mind was capable of appreciating to the full those distinctions which, by the vulgar, are not so much as suspected. Admitted to equal converse with men and women who represented the best in English society, he could cast away the evil grudge, the fierce spirit of self-assertion, and be what nature had proposed in endowing him....
>
> A bee hummed past him, and this sound...filled his heart to overflowing. Moisture made his eyes dim, and at the impulse of a feeling of gratitude, such as only the subtlest care of psychology could fully have explained, he turned to Buckland, saying:
>
> "But for my meeting with you I should have had a lonely and not very cheerful holiday. I owe you a great deal." (160–61)

Peak's tears and his gratitude require close attention because, despite appearances, they are not sincere. They stem from Peak's apprehension of what he might be in such a setting, and are deformed by his intense self-pity, which quickly re-emerges in the familiar form of resentment. We cannot trust his gratitude or his tears or his admiration for the English country house; though seemingly genuine, his adulation repels us because it calls forth such a mixed response from Peak.

There is a suggestion, too, that even in this moment of apparent gratitude, Peak is already instinctively manipulating his hosts by his pathetic appeal. Admiration, envy, contempt, resentment—the emotions wash over Peak's consciousness until he can no longer sound himself. In Martin Warricombe's study he watches himself, knowing "insincerity must be very careful if it would not jar upon his refined ear" (165). He guards his speech lest it sound "too much like flattery. . . . Resurgent envy gave him no little trouble. . . . 'How easy for a man to do notable work amid such surroundings!'" he reflects, and how difficult it is to judge this mixture of petty self-excuse and legitimate observation. Still later that evening Peak's artful pretense of candor and his open appeal as a social inferior to a superior for patronage completely disarm the suspicious Buckland, whose own liberal posturings have not fooled Peak for a minute.

Throughout the day Peak's intellect and emotions remain too sharply divided to permit a consistent view of himself or a consistent evaluation of his surroundings or of his actions. "Godwin, as he sat in the drawing-room and enjoyed its atmosphere of refinement, sincerely held himself of far more account as an intellectual being than all the persons about him." Does he not then deserve to be included in the world of affluent decorum which he is uniquely capable of appreciating?

> He was now playing the conscious hypocrite; not a pleasant thing to face and accept, but the fault was not his—fate had brought it about. At all events, he aimed at no vulgar profit; his own desire was for human fellowship; he sought nothing but that solace which every code of morals has deemed legitimate. Let the society which compelled to such an expedient bear the burden of its shame. (169)

Yet by nightfall Peak wonders: "What fatal power had subdued him? What extraordinary influence had guided his tongue, constrained his features? His conscious self had had no part in all this comedy; now for the first time was he taking count of the character he had played" (178). Further rationalization only leads him to deplore "the ancestral vice in his blood, brought out by over-tempting circumstance. The long line of baseborn predecessors, the grovelling hinds and mechanics of his genealogy, were responsible for this. Oh for a name wherewith honour was hereditary!" (179). If this passage strikes us as the grossest shirking of personal responsibility, the most degrading form of class-consciousness, we should remember that it is not just Peak who speaks this way about breeding; the narrator of *Demos* takes the matter of hereditary determinism quite as seriously.

These shifts from self-satisfaction to self-justification to self-condemnation are only the beginning of Peak's torment about his hypocrisy. All his positions are poses, graspings after a stable identity, while the disintegration of his consciousness goes on apace. This admirer of the honest soul defends himself before Earwaker arguing: "Honest? Honest? Who is or can be honest? Who truly declares himself?" (194). Peak's motto is *"Foris ut moris, intus ut libet,"* but inwardly he experiences "a tormenting metaphysical doubt of his own identity" (252).[8]

*   *   *

Throughout his career Peak serves as a mirror of society, reflecting the class-consciousness, the hypocrisy, the compromises and insincerities essential to its continuance. The sophistry this skeptic practices on himself is only an extreme form of the sort of intellectual compromise which he had attacked in his article, so that he is neither better nor worse than the "society which compelled [him] to such an expedient." Sidwell herself comes to recognize that "English society at large made profession of a faith which in no sense whatever it could be said sincerely to hold.... Was there not every reason to believe that thousands of people keep up an ignoble formalism, because they feared the social results of declaring their severance from the religion of the churches?" she asks (392). Others protect privilege with hypocrisy. Is Peak any worse in pretending to a formalism which insures his admission to that privileged world? The novel cannot answer this question, but simply in posing it Gissing makes us aware of the role of ideology in preserving hegemony.

In his clerical career Peak has an upper-class double, Bruno Chilvers, the aristocratic dandy who beats out Peak on Prize Day at Whitelaw and who is destined to win in the game of imposture as well. As a cleric eager to make a name for himself by keeping up with the times, Chilvers professes a Christianity so broad that it makes all of Peak's belated "conscientious scruples about entering the Church...superfluous" (353). "What were this man's real opinions?" Peak wonders. "Vanity, no doubt, was his prime motive, but did it operate to make a cleric of a secret materialist, or to incite a display of excessive liberalism in one whose convictions were orthodox?" Buckland Warricombe recognizes that "anyone who had personal reasons might treat Chilvers precisely as I have treated Peak. Both of them may be honest. Yet in Peak's case all appearances are against him—just because he is of low birth, has no means, and wants desperately to get into society" (375).

Peak's masquerade exposes the hollowness of Buckland's political liberalism and his egalitarian sentiments. After he has unmasked Peak, Buckland rants at Sidwell:

> [Peak] has somehow got the exterior of a gentleman; you could not believe that one who behaved so agreeably and talked so well was concealing an essentially base nature. But I must remind you that Peak belongs by origin to the lower classes, which is as much to say that he lacks the sense of honour generally inherited by men of our world. A powerful intellect by no means implies a corresponding development of the moral sense. (380)

Buckland's marriage to a tanner's daughter at the end of the novel provides an ironic parallel to Peak's failed courtship (and to the spinsterhood he forces on his sister), but his choice does not lead him to a new degree of self-consciousness. By contrast with Chilvers and Buckland, Peak stands as a reflective, self-aware man, whose conscience is sharpened by experience—a man whose designs and disgrace are caused by the class structure rather than by a defective standard of personal integrity.

Buckland's genial father, Martin Warricombe, who had relied on Peak to reconcile science and dogma for him, finds he is able to defer forever that thorough investigation which would destroy his honest soul. "His life, indeed, was one of debate postponed" (228). Most strikingly, Sidwell herself, that ideal of refined womanhood which fascinated Gissing as well as Peak, seems compromised when she chooses, in her words, "comfort" and "respectability" instead of life with Peak, whom she passionately loves. Although her religious beliefs are no longer an obstacle to their union, she lacks "the courage" to "dare to act upon her best impulses. . . . I am bound to a certain sphere of life. The fact that I have outgrown it, counts for nothing. . . . To act as I wish would be to outrage every rule and prejudice of the society to which I belong" (490).[9]

Peak's feelings about Sidwell are as divided as the rest of his consciousness; the habit of analysis makes him uncertain about his love. As his ideal, she stimulates in him an uncomfortable sense of his own baseness, and he is inclined to resent her even as he pursues her. He begins their penultimate interview, when he proposes, feeling that "he has come here to act a part, and that the end of the interview, be it what it might, would only affect him superficially" (360); in the course of the interview he does play many parts, speaking at first with "a rough arrogance [which] sounded like deliberate rudeness." But the effort to keep her at a distance gives way to "an impulse of unimpaired sincerity," and Peak confesses his love, adding, "I want you to know me." The consciousness that he is deceiving her even as he speaks "sincerely" makes Peak contemptuous of himself *and* her. "Why had she not intelligence enough to see through the hypocrisy, which at times was so thin a veil? How defective must her sympathy be!" He finds himself beginning a confession, appealing to her sympathy for a man "born in exile." Then he abruptly halts, and almost by way of testing—or punishing—the "utterly unsuspecting" Sidwell, who cannot "realise his character and his temptations," he asks her to marry him. At the end of the interview he continues to find himself trapped in his own words; when he reminds her that he is "seeking for a livelihood as well as for a sphere of usefulness," his eyes fall as he recognizes that he has left the door open for her to comment on her dowry. "The thought revived his painful self-consciousness; it was that of a schemer, yet would not the curse of poverty have suggested it to any man?" (365). Peak's class-consciousness intensifies his divisive self-consciousness, which no acceptance by an honest soul can possibly heal.

Having wooed Sidwell with the conventional deference of a poor man, Peak accepts passively her brother's accusations of dishonor and baseness; in their last interview he enters bowed with shame, accepting her "noble" or we might say her normative perspective. But in this moment of degradation, he offers in his defense a new definition of sincerity in which "self-examination" replaces the old-fashioned "freedom from falsification and dissimulation."[10]

Peak begins by speaking in the terms of the honest soul, wondering how Sidwell could love him when he is so "unlovable," so lacking in "the gift of pleasing—moral grace"; he then tries to describe his character.

> "My strongest emotions seem to be absorbed in revolt; for once that I feel tenderly, I have a hundred fierce, resentful, tempestuous moods. To be suave and smiling in common intercourse costs me an effort. I have to act the part, and this habit makes me sceptical, whenever I am really prompted to gentleness. I criticise myself ceaselessly; expose without mercy all those characteristics which another man would keep out of sight. Yes, and for this very reason, just because I think myself unlovable—the gift of love means far more to me than to other men. If you could conceive the passion of gratitude which possessed me for hours after I left you the other day!...
>
> In comparison with this sincerity, what becomes of the pretence you blame in me? If you knew how paltry it seems—that accusation of dishonesty!" (404–5)

This has something of the tone and method of argument of Dostoevsky's Underground Man—something, too, of his perversity. Peak's sense of self, acute but disintegrated, compels him to probe, to analyze, to expose what other men keep hidden. Unpleasant and resentful as he is, he stands in positive contrast to the honest soul whose failure to know itself has made it bland and flabby when it is not actually corrupt. While Peak's hypocrisy has occasioned a continual self-examination, society's is a cultivated blindness. The intensity of Peak's self-consciousness, which destroys the possibility of sincerity, pushes him toward a distinct experience of selfhood achieved not in spite of, but because of, his self-division, self-contempt, and resentment.

*   *   *

Jacob Korg notes that after Gissing finished the manuscript of *Born in Exile*, he "recorded in his diary a decision to change his [protagonist's] name from 'Peak' to 'Peek,' as though he were not sure whether his character embodied the lofty nobility of the former or the hideous furtiveness of the latter."[11] Gissing's difficulty in judging Peak stems from the fact that through this character he confronted some acute contradictions within bourgeois ideology, contradictions implicit in his own adoption of conservative values. Gazing from below on the heights of distinction in a class-bound society makes one necessarily a furtive voyeur, and climbing those peaks exposes one as an imposter. Even where it authorizes upward mobility, ideology defines those on the lower slopes as inferiors; climbing, motivated by envy and resentment, betrays one's inherent baseness. The individual is powerless to develop himself, to reach those desirable peaks—unless it be by that difficult path which Hegel proposed, the base self's journey through disintegration. Although he had created Peak, Gissing resisted acknowledging the new moral possibilities of the base self, just as he resisted exposing directly the oppressiveness and intolerability of the class structure. During the composition of this novel and even after its completion, he was tempted to judge his character once and for all by the norm of the honest soul.

And yet this norm has been so obviously undermined in the course of the novel. Consider in the following passage how seriously both Peak and his ideals are compromised. At the Warricombes Peak reflects: "This English home, was it not surely the best result of civilization in an age devoted to material progress? Here was peace, here was scope for the kindliest emotions" (170). Such a setting would "humanise" him, Peak thinks, and then admits:

> Nothing easier than to condemn the mode of life represented by this wealthy middle class; but compare it with other existences conceivable by a thinking man, and it was emphatically good. It aimed at placidity, at benevolence, at supreme cleanliness,—things which more than compensated for the absence of higher spirituality. (170–71)

This is surely a milquetoast ideal. Peak as much as says that the noble world has been drained of all value as an ideal; it is simply more comfortable compared with the life of materially disadvantaged classes. Despite Peak's conscious intention to praise, the noble world betrays its affinity with the unexceptional, the comfortable, the merely inoffensive. As for the honest souls nurtured here, Peak reflects with an ironic blend of condescension and envy:

> We can be but what we are; these people accepted themselves, and in so doing became estimable mortals. No imbecile pretensions exposed them to the rebuke of a social satirist; no vulgarity tainted their familiar intercourse. Their allegiance to a worn-out creed was felt as an added grace; thus only could their souls aspire, and the imperfect poetry of their natures be developed. (171)

"We can be but what we are," Peak observes, but he has never lived by that notion. "We can be what we are not": that possibility is at the root of his ambition to achieve a "self"; an idea of freedom inspires his hypocrisy. The honest souls nurtured here are not "estimable mortals" but intellectually lazy, protected people who remain comfortable by avoiding rigorous self-scrutiny. Peak's story exposes this ideal although he and his author stop short of the conscious recognition of their devaluation. We do not have "the rebuke of a social satirist" but rather the disturbing silence of "blank irony" which withholds judgment on what should be judged.[12]

Peak's snobbery and class-consciousness, his imitation of Tory sentiments and his adoption of Tory values, amount to an unconsciously hostile mimicry which in spite of himself betrays his resentment and exposes the vacuousness of that upper-middle class he seeks to enter. Yet Gissing himself has expressed reactionary views similar to Peak's in other works. Might we ascribe a similarly hostile, unconscious intention to Gissing? A comparison with an earlier novel *Demos* allows us to see how in *Born in Exile* Gissing gave the screw an extra turn to expose contradictions in his own ideological situation. Peak is in many ways similar to the plebian Richard Mutimer who pursues and eventually marries the well-bred Adela Waltham after convincing her to adopt his socialist views. Mutimer is unquestionably her inferior in every respect, and eventually the folly of her egalitarianism is revealed to Adela in the physiognomy of her sleeping husband.

> What was the meaning now first revealed to her in that countenance? The features had a massive regularity; there was nothing grotesque, nothing on the surface repulsive; yet, beholding the face as if it were that of a man unknown to her, she felt that a whole world of natural antipathies was between it and her.
> It was the face of a man by birth and breeding altogether beneath her.
> Never had she understood that as now.... He was not of her class, not of her world; only by violent wrenching of the laws of nature had they come together. She had spent years in trying to convince herself that there were no such distinctions, that only an unworthy prejudice parted class from class. One moment of true insight was worth more than all her theorising on abstract principles. To be her equal, this man must be born again.[13]

Adela is the moral center of the novel, and since these views are nowhere qualified and indeed are confirmed by the action, which shows Mutimer to be grossly mistaken at every point, we may suppose that the narrator of this novel, like Peak, accepts "a true distinction of social classes [based on] hereditary social standing." We may be repelled, but the novel's ideological perspective is straightforward. Mutimer's aggression against the established order is evident in his political stance, and his punishment leaves that order secure.

Peak's aggression is similarly punished, but unlike Mutimer, Peak is not an opponent but a defender of the social hierarchy. Ideologically he is close to the disinherited gentleman Eldon who eventually marries Adela; thus Peak's punishment for his presumption is a paradoxical way of reaffirming the established order. We may wonder whether, as a conservative spokesman, he has somehow misrepresented the values of the elite, but his speech to Earwaker supporting a social hierarchy based on birth says crudely what the narrator of *Demos* puts only slightly less overtly. His discomfitingly reductive view of religious dogma as a police force is echoed later in the novel by Sidwell, who corresponds to the idealized figure of Adela Waltham. As an articulator of conservative ideology, Peak seems reliable; that is, he seems to express authorial values.

Nevertheless, Peak's values are disturbing, and not merely because they are repugnant to a liberal reader. The text itself obliges us to recognize how self-defeating such values are when the baseborn Peak appropriates them. No matter how enthusiastic his advocacy of a social elite, Peak must always be excluded from it. The incongruities between Peak and his snobbish class-consciousness cause the reader to be aware that his values are peculiar to a privileged elite; we are bound to see them as ideological weapons which help to maintain the hegemony of a class from which Peak is excluded.[14]

The end of *Born in Exile* appears to confirm Gissing's conservative view of the class structure; as in *Demos,* the impostor is exposed, and the social hierarchy is left intact. But in this novel the impostor defends the legitimacy of a social hierarchy that excludes him; he is an embarrassing advocate of values which Gissing elsewhere affirms. In *Born in Exile* Gissing doesn't simply produce another straightforward, ideologically conservative novel about the inalterability of the class structure. By combining character types which heretofore he had kept quite separate—the Milvains and Reardons, the Mutimers and Eldons—Gissing exposes central contradictions within bourgeois ideology and explores them in the double bind situation of Peak (Peek?), who is both the unscrupulous adventurer and the Tory dreamer. Through his alter ego, Gissing expressed in a covert way his own resentment of a class structure which was deeply attractive but desperately damaging to himself. Peak's snobbery, which is both aggressive and self-destructive, reflects the punitive way in which Gissing's own class-consciousness operated, carrying a built-in punishment for the resentment he harbored.

Figure 2. Thomas Hardy at 34 or 35
(Thomas Hardy Memorial Collection in the Dorset County Museum, Dorchester, Dorset)

2

Hardy: The Strange Continuator

Down there I seem to be false to myself, my simple self that was,
And is not now, and I see him watching, wondering what crass
   cause
Can have merged him into such a strange continuator as this,
Who yet has something in common with himself, my chrysalis.
                                        "Wessex Heights" (1896)

Hardy wrote "Wessex Heights" a year after the publication of *Jude the Obscure*. The mood of depression and alienation which links "Wessex Heights" to the "In Tenebris" poems of the same year is generally supposed to have been occasioned by the public outcry against what was to be his last novel and by his growing estrangement from his wife, who had attempted to stop publication of *Jude*. In "Wessex Heights" Hardy imagines himself turning his back on his critics—on Emma, on the optimists he satirizes in "In Tenebris II," and on the detractors of "Jude the Obscene," the "men with a wintry sneer, and women with tart disparagings"—and climbing one of those hills "where men have never cared to haunt." He hopes to gain some perspective on the present by returning to his native ground.[1] But at the root of Hardy's estrangement is his consciousness of a self-division, which causes him to feel "shadowed" or "haunted" by his past. From the vantage point of a Wessex hill he observes, "Down there I seem to be false to myself, my simple self that was,/ And is not now...." Along with his other critics, this "simple self" watches Hardy, wondering what chance—what "crass cause"—has "merged him into such a strange continuator as this." The presence of this "chrysalis" self from which the "I" of the poem has emerged is a constant stimulus to memory; the consciousness of his own metamorphosis inspires the successive stanzas in which Hardy is troubled by several specters from his past, the first two of whom may be avatars of Tess and Jude.

   Virtually everyone is conscious of a distinction between his present self and the "simple self" of his youth, but only a few feel "false" to themselves, and fewer still are continually haunted by this double consciousness. While outwardly Hardy had successfully negotiated a dramatic social advancement, inwardly he felt a prolonged, wrenching break with his past. He was born in 1840, the son of a domestic servant and a mason in a tiny hamlet in Dorsetshire. His parents kept him at school until he was sixteen, two years longer than was customary, and then apprenticed him to an architect in Dorchester. Both facts suggest that his parents, and probably his mother in particular, hoped that their son would be upwardly mobile. At twenty-one Hardy went up to London to work in an architect's office; he continued a substantial program of self-education and began to look seriously to writing as a career best suited to his talents and education. His first novel, never published, was entitled *The Poor Man and the Lady; By the Poor Man* (1867) and was based in part on his experience as a country youth fully aware of class distinctions in mid-century London. Hardy later described his novel as:

> ... a sweeping dramatic satire of the squirearchy and nobility, London society, the vulgarity of the middle class, modern Christianity, church-restoration, and political and domestic morals in general, the author's views, in fact being obviously those of a young man with a passion for reforming the world ... the tendency of the writing being socialistic, not to say revolutionary.... [2]

Being advised by George Meredith not to "'nail his colours to the mast' so definitely in a first book, if he wished to do anything practical in literature," (LWTH, 62) Hardy turned to the rural world of his youth and produced four novels in as many years: *Desperate Remedies* (1871), *Under the Greenwood Tree* (1872), *A Pair of Blue Eyes* (1873), and *Far from the Madding Crowd* (1874). Even in these pastoral novels, Hardy continued to return to issues raised in his first work, in particular to the experience of social mobility among the working and lower-middle classes. His own social advancement was confirmed by his marriage to a "lady," Emma Gifford, whose connections with a professional world (daughter of a lawyer, niece of a clergyman) raised her high in her own and in Hardy's esteem. Emma was always conscious of having married beneath her station and was never on close terms with Hardy's parents. After marriage, Hardy curtailed his social connections with the working-class friends and relatives of his youth, excepting his immediate family. He continued his career as a novelist, dividing his time between Dorset and London, where his eminence as a writer gave him entrée into upper-middle-class circles which made Emma's social pretentions look provincial. The marriage was not altogether happy, and social strains together with the increasing candor of his fiction added to their estrangement. When Emma died in 1912, Hardy had published only three of the eight volumes of poetry which were to add to his reputation. When he died in 1928 and was buried in Westminster Abbey, he was considered to be the unofficial poet laureate of England.[3]

In his own day Hardy was appreciated chiefly as the chronicler of a timeless, pastoral world, a regional novelist whose philosophical pessimism lent a tragic resonance to his work. To his readers, Wessex was remote: an imaginary world which had almost nothing to do with contemporary social experience. Yet the social mobility of the middle and lower classes which was continuing to change English society was a constant theme in Hardy's fiction, and his novels are, as Raymond Williams observes, "increasingly concerned with change." He puts at the center of his fiction "exposed and separated individuals [who are] only the most developed cases of a general exposure and separation," characters like Tess or Grace Melbury, Clym Yeobright or Henchard, each of whom is unclassed by education or ambition. Irving Howe comments on this same theme.

> For [Hardy] the prospect of social change is inseparable from the threat of personal displacement, and the two together stir up in his work a constant—though extremely fruitful—discord of approval and anxiety.... It is correct to say, as does John Holloway, that in Hardy's world 'the great disaster for an individual is to be deraciné'; but to say this and no more, is not to say enough. For in his best novels, turning sharply away from Wordsworth and the whole nature mystique, Hardy becomes emotionally entangled with such rebellious figures as Clym Yeobright and Jude Fawley, who decide to separate themselves from their environment and pay the price of estrangement. Hardy believes in the virtues of passivity, but... his strongest creative energies are stirred by the assertiveness of men defining themselves apart from and in opposition to the natural order [and, I would add, the social order]. At the end he draws away from them and must punish their claims to self-sufficiency, yet in his heart of hearts he loves them.[4]

Hardy's preoccupation with the theme of social change, his ambivalence, and the sympathy he feels for his rebels, outcasts, and unclassed figures are grounded in his personal experience of deracination, which is most fully registered in his last novel. *Jude the Obscure* is a meditation on his youthful ambition; it is a return to the concerns of his first, unpublished novel, a qualified attempt to "nail his colours to the mast"; and it is an attempt to recall and reassess the "simple self that was" in order to understand his strange continuation.

*   *   *

There is in Hardy's fiction a recurring protagonist, a problematically superior poor man, possessed of unusual sensibility or ambition, who comes to feel that he is "born out of due time," as Hardy says of himself in "In Tenebris II." The humble world of his birth cannot nourish his talent or provide scope for his aspiration. A passive man, he is tempted to retreat from the world and spurn competition, but he overcomes this timidity and attempts to raise himself socially. He is, as Hardy says of Jude, "a species of Dick Whittington whose spirit [is] touched to finer issues than a mere material gain."[5] He seeks material advantages as a means to growth and self-development; his social mobility is a psychological quest for identity and a spiritual quest for freedom. However, his attempt to enlarge himself involves him in some deception, secrecy, or betrayal which compromises his integrity. Gradually he becomes aware that his development entails his alienation.

Hardy's attitude toward this character changes as he reassesses the experience of upward mobility. Certainly Will *Strong,* the hero of *The Poor Man and the Lady,* must have been the most naive, optimistic version of this *Hardy* protagonist, though it is interesting to note that even in this earliest work the "lady" dies the moment she is won; the hero's success is fleeting. *The Hand of Ethelberta,* written in 1876 shortly after Hardy's marriage, is virtually a roman à clef about his social rise and his continuing anxiety about his connections with a lower-class world of servants, laborers, and small tradesmen.[6] The daughter of a butler, Ethelberta Chickerel is a governess for a gentry family and runs off with the oldest son; when he dies, she is adopted by his mother and transformed into a lady. To keep her social position and to play her "hand" so as to marry well again, Ethelberta is obliged to conceal her own family connections. She refuses to allow her affections to be engaged by her poor but worthy lover and eventually lands a debauched old viscount; she ends her career happily enough managing his large estate.

The elements of betrayal and deception, treated lightly in *The Hand of Ethelberta,* are the basis for tragedy in the story of Michael Henchard who, by selling his wife and daughter, gains the freedom he needs to pull himself up from day laborer to mayor of Casterbridge. Try as he will, he cannot right the wrong done in the past, and the twenty-year-old secret contributes in a variety of ways to his social and financial decline. Hardy returns to the idea that ambition involves betrayal in *The Woodlanders,* written in 1887, a year after *The Mayor of Casterbridge.* Melbury's desire that his daughter Grace become a lady leads him to break his unspoken promise that Winterborne shall marry her. She is sent away to school and returns a demonstrably unsuitable wife for a laboring man. Instead she is paired off with Dr. Fitzpiers, whose social rootlessness, like Grace's own, is linked to his incapacity for fidelity. When the faithful Winterborne dies, Grace is doomed to a loveless marriage.

Nor can the poor man avoid disillusionment and self-betrayal by denying his ambition. In *The Return of the Native* (1878) Clym Yeobright gives up a successful career as a diamond merchant in Paris, but his return to Egdon

Heath in order to become a schoolteacher is a form of blindness, the metaphor made literal in the novel. In spite of, indeed because of, his altruism, Clym betrays his mother, Eustacia, and himself. In his naive underestimation of the consequences of social mobility and his ultimately selfish yearning to identify with a lower social group, Clym is similar to Walter Egremont, Gissing's idealist in *Thyrza*.

While mobility was a time-honored theme when Hardy began writing, in his fiction for the first time it regularly provides the basis for tragedy. His protagonist is caught in a double bind created by the wish to develop his potential. Pursuing his aspirations at the expense of connection to family and community, he feels guilty for breaking with a class to which he is already uncertainly related by virtue of those aspirations. That guilt is heightened by his consciousness of moving into an opposing, sometimes antagonistic class, which is obliged to shore up its privilege against the increasing pressure for democracy, a class which is obliged to exclude, to sneer, and to wear blinders to maintain its power and prestige. It is, nevertheless, the educated class, albeit a class defensively guarding education and cultivation as its special preserve, the very basis of its legitimacy. Recognizing all this, the poor man is estranged from both social milieux.

The figure behind this protagonist is Hardy himself, and I argue that his experience of upward mobility was an important factor underlying his philosophical pessimism. In his fiction the frustrations of his particular social experience are sometimes reconceived as aspects of the universal human condition; the social double bind is translated into a philosophical one. This process of expanding, but also of disguising, his personal experience is clearest in *Jude the Obscure*. There the frustration and disillusionment which accompany social mobility are seen as the fate of all men in a world which is not designed to nurture man's higher instincts, a world in which nature "exceed[ed] her mission... when she crossed the line from invertebrates to vertebrates" (LWTH, 227). At the outset of his career Hardy composed this "Young Man's Epigram on Existence."

> A senseless school, where we must give
> Our lives that we may learn to live!
> A dolt is he who memorizes
> Lessons that leave no time for prizes.

And in 1885 he captured in a phrase the futility of wisdom: "Experience *un*teaches" (LWTH, 182). In Hardy's tragic Bildungsroman Jude's education makes him wise by showing him there is no way to use his potential; the story of his struggle to develop suggests that the game is not worth the candle. Hardy's consciousness of this philosophical no-win situation was part of his mental and emotional baggage from his earliest days as a poor man in London; it was not significantly affected by his reading of Darwin or Schopenhauer or, on the other hand, by his outwardly successful career.

*   *   *

Possibly the work that most reveals the strain of this author's deracination is *The Life and Work of Thomas Hardy,* which appeared in two volumes after his death under his second wife's name. It was in fact largely ghost-written by Hardy himself and is quite literally an "authorized biography," an effort to control what the public would know and think about Thomas Hardy. In this alternately diffident and blasé success story, the protagonist is another curious version of the poor man who married a lady and became a famous Victorian author. There is no doubt that to some degree the biography was a conscious deception: Hardy burned his notes for it every evening after Mrs. Hardy had typed up his recollections in the third person. It may also have been in part an unconscious deception, reflecting a desire to edit the past in order to better harmonize it with the present, to cull certain discordant memories and to repress the ambivalences Hardy felt as a result of moving between two worlds. But in spite of Hardy's effort to conceal the magnitude of his social rise, *The Life* reveals a good deal about that experience indirectly. It is not a simple document. Hardy represents his family and background in such a way as to close the distance between himself and his middle-class readers, and he does not stint in recording his social engagements among the upper-middle class once he had become a celebrated author. But the patchwork surface of *The Life,* including diary entries, philosophical notations, letters, anecdotes, and narrative, also allows Hardy to make candid (sometimes barbed) remarks about the social structure without following them up. One has the impression of a man acutely aware of class distinctions but determined not to say too much unkind about them. Finally *The Life* suggests that Hardy wished to project the image of an entirely unambitious man who scarcely noticed and who certainly did not pursue his own success. It is entirely possible that Hardy sincerely saw himself in this way. However, such a self-image would have been an understandable way of dealing with ideological contradictions about social mobility.[7]

Hardy begins *The Life* with an idea that was obviously imaginatively important to him, the notion that his family had "declined" from distinguished ancestors, including a "Thomas le Hardy" who had come to Dorset from Jersey in the fifteenth century. As a consequence his people "had the characteristics of an old family of spent social energies, that were revealed even in the Thomas Hardy of this memoir (as in his father and grandfather), who had never cared to take advantage of the many worldly opportunities that his popularity and esteem as an author afforded him" (LWTH, 9). The passage makes claim to an ancestry which offsets the quite humble social status of his parents and grounds in heredity Hardy's lack of ambition.

In presenting his immediate family background, Hardy stresses his father's status as an independent mason who hired workmen in his business, his mother's and grandmother's love of reading, his father's association with the parish choir—matters of which he was understandably proud. He alludes only slightly or not at all to experiences which would have disclosed the family's economic vulnerability, such as the fact that his mother was raised on parish relief and went out to work as a domestic servant at an early age. Almost more important than the facts he chooses to include is the narrating voice of *The Life*. By ghosting his biography, Hardy avoided the intimate, first-person voice of a man recalling his childhood and assumed the role of a detached, disinterested observer who could write of Hardy's birthplace as a "quaint domicile," the latinate word suggesting the educated distance from which the house appears "quaint" as it would to Hardy's urban audience. By controlling both the material and the manner of presenting his origins, Hardy made his background seem alternately picturesque and unexceptional. From *The Life* we get little sense of the imperative to maintain and indeed improve upon the family's independent status, little sense of the obstacles to a young boy's dream of entering the Church or going up to Oxford.

What we have instead is a portrait of the artist as an unusually passive boy, the kind of boy we will meet again in Paul Morel. Both Hardy and Lawrence had mothers who nurtured their ambition; indeed it may not be too much to say that their mothers demanded that the sons achieve something beyond the conventional expectations of the father's social class. And Hardy's father seems to have been in some respects like Walter Morel—a personable, easygoing man who was quite content with his social circumstances. One anecdote from *The Life*, which has a close parallel in *Jude the Obscure*, suggests how Hardy may have reacted to his mother's pressure to make something of himself.

> He was lying on his back in the sun, thinking how useless he was, and covered his face with his straw hat. The sun's rays streamed through the interstices of the straw, the lining having disappeared. Reflecting on his experiences of the world so far as he had got, he came to the conclusion that he did not wish to grow up. Other boys were always talking of when they would be men; he did not want at all to be a man, or to possess things, but to remain as he was, in the same spot, and to know no more people than he already knew (about half a dozen). Yet this early evidence of that lack of social ambition which followed him through life was shown when he was in perfect health and happy circumstances. (LWTH, 20)

The appeal of living within a small community and cheerfully accepting its limitations is powerful, and there is every reason to believe that Hardy felt its allure and believed he was in many ways his father's child. However, bringing this memory forth as "*evidence* of a lack of a social ambition" suggests that he feels he must insist on his passivity, and indeed we find him doing this at several points. In 1867, when Hardy was working for Blomfield's architectural firm in London and trying to find an appropriate career for himself, *The Life* records: "[Hardy] constitutionally shrank from the business of social advancement, caring for life as an emotion rather than for life as a science of climbing, in which respect he was quizzed by his acquaintance for his lack of ambition" (LWTH, 54). Although inwardly Hardy must have shrunk "from the business of social advancement," outwardly he was actively working to move beyond his father's social class. In presenting himself as innately unambitious, he both registers his own ambivalence about rising and avoids the risk of being judged by the world as a social climber.

Quite late in *The Life* Hardy again urges his lack of ambition, this time in connection with his career as a poet.

> In a United States periodical...it was stated that "Thomas Hardy is a realistic novelist who...has a grim determination to go down to posterity wearing the laurels of a poet." This writer was a glaring illustration of the danger of reading motives into action. Of course there was no "grim determination," no thought of "laurels." Thomas Hardy was always a person with an unconscious, or rather unreasoning, *tendency,* and the poetic tendency had been his from the earliest. He would tell that it used to be said to him at Sir Arthur Blomfield's: "Hardy, there can hardly have been anybody in the world with less ambition than you." At this time the real state of his mind was, in his own words, that "A sense of the truth of poetry, of its supreme place in literature, had awakened itself in me. At the risk of ruining all my worldly prospects I dabbled in it...was forced out of it.... It came back upon me.... All was of the nature of being led by a mood, without foresight, or regard to whither it led." (LWTH, 415)

The idea of an unconscious "tendency," of "being led by a mood," implies that Hardy's success and his art came effortlessly to one innately unambitious. The phrase "forced out" is the only hint of the hardships endured in his difficult decade, 1865–75, during which only the "grim determination" of the author led him to fiction (and hence to "worldly" success) and saw him through the setbacks, rejections, and partial successes of these early years. But effort must have no place in his story.

Let me stress that I do not mean to impugn Hardy's sincerity. My point is that his passivity was a psychological response to the pressure to rise and to the ambivalence he felt about rising; the conviction about his passivity allowed him to continue in a career which brought social advancement without feeling the stigma of being a social climber. This particular psychological response is useful to identify when we come to Jude, in whom we see the debilitating effect of passivity.

While *The Life* suggests that in many respects Hardy wished to mute for his readership his humble origins and the strain of rising into the middle class, at several points he asserts his class difference and connects the value of his writing to the fact that he comes from "below." The point is made in a diary entry of 1866, recorded in *The Life:* "The defects of a class are more perceptible to the class immediately below it than to itself" (LWTH, 56). In an entry from 1888 Hardy observes: "The literary productions of men of rigidly good family and rigidly correct education, mostly treat social conventions and contrivances—the artificial forms of living—as if they were cardinal facts of life" (LWTH, 222). In both entries, the value to a writer of a perspective "from below" is carefully stated as a generalization, but the relevance to Hardy is clear; handicaps such as his self-education or family background become unique advantages, permitting him to see through "artificial forms" to "cardinal facts of life." In 1890, after recording that the manuscript of *Tess* is finished, Hardy notes:

> "Met Mrs. T. and her great eyes in a corner of the rooms, as if washed up by the surging crowd. The most beautiful woman present.... But these women! If put into rough wrappers in a turnip-field, where would their beauty be?"...
>
> He observes later in respect of such scenes as these: "Society, *collectively,* has neither seen what any ordinary person can see, read what every ordinary person has read, nor thought what every ordinary person has thought." (LWTH, 235)

Without drawing attention to his own social background, Hardy again maintains that middle-class status amounts to a set of blinders which hides "ordinary" experiences of other classes; his own movement up from below again becomes a secret advantage instead of a liability.

Hardy had urged a similar claim about the value of his work in his 1868 letter to publisher Alexander MacMillan about *The Poor Man and the Lady.*

> In writing the novel...the following considerations had place.
>
> That the upper classes of society have been induced to read, before any, books in which *they themselves* are painted by a comparative outsider.
>
> That in works of such a kind, unmitigated utterances of strong feeling against the class to which these readers belong, may lead them to throw down a volume in disgust; whilst the very same feelings inserted edgewise so to say; half concealed beneath ambiguous expressions, or at any rate written as if they were not the chief aims of the book (even though they may be)—become the most attractive remarks of all.
>
> That now a days, discussions on the questions of manners, rising in the world, &c (the main incidents of the novel) have grown to be particularly absorbing....
>
> That novelty of *position* and *view* in relation to a known subject, is more taking among the readers of light literature than even absolute novelty of subject.[8]

It becomes a hallmark of Hardy to insert his hostile feelings about the class structure "edgewise...half concealed beneath ambiguous expressions...as if they were not the chief aims of the book," the implication of this letter being that they were. This describes a strategy in *The Life,* in his first novel, and in *Jude,* all of which offer a critical perspective on the middle classes as they are seen from "below." Hardy understood that this perspective contributed to the value of his work even though he would often be at pains to disguise or deny his criticisms.

The Life developed about equally the images of Hardy as a collector of quaint or grotesque anecdotes, Hardy the writer and thinker, and Hardy the clubman, moving easily from one social gathering to the next. It is riddled with evasions, contradictions, and ironies which suggest both the hostility and the attraction which Hardy felt for the upper-middle class. His strained relationship with "Society" is evident in the following passage from *The Life,* which begins with a 1915 diary entry in which Hardy had noted: "I fear I have always been considered the Dark Horse of contemporary English literature." The tone is one of good-humored resignation about general opinion which persists in seeing him as a "dark horse"; the "biographer" then goes on to other matters, returning to the remark after several paragraphs.

> The above note on his being considered a Dark Horse was apt enough, when it is known that none of the society men who met him suspected from his simple manner the potentialities of observation that were in him. This unassertive air, unconsciously worn, served him as an invisible coat almost to uncanniness. At the houses and clubs where he encountered other writers and critics and world-practised readers of character, whose bearing towards him was often as towards one who did not reach their altitudes, he was seeing through them as though they were glass. He set down some cutting and satirical notes on their qualities and compass, but destroyed all of them, not wishing to leave behind him anything which could be deemed a gratuitous belittling of others. (LWTH, 408)

It is the "biographer" rather than the Hardy of the diary entry who makes us aware of the "dark horse" as a metaphor for concealed greatness—hidden competitor and unsuspected winner—and who also makes us aware that Hardy is a "dark horse" because of his class. The condescension of the establishment to "the good little Thomas Hardy," as Henry James called him, is exposed and serves as a foil for Hardy's artistic and moral superiority. Without alluding directly to the social hierarchy, Hardy implies that because he is from "below," he can see through "as though they were glass" those above who snub him. Confident of their superior social position, these "other writers and critics and world-practised readers of character" fail to see Hardy's advantage, his "potentialities of observation." His "simple," "unassertive" manner, "unconsciously worn" makes him the more reliable perceiver. The use of four negating prefixes in one sentence reflects both Hardy's diffidence and the way in which the negative becomes the positive, the disadvantage, the advantage in Hardy's view. But the oblique admission of social snubs and the complicated line of defense are a measure of the strain with which Hardy maintained his position between two worlds.

The Life was one of Hardy's responses to the double bind of upward mobility; it testifies to his desire to conceal the extent of that rise and to establish his connection with the upper-middle class. The unambitious persona was an essential self-image which distinguished Hardy (as it would Jude) from the pushy, upwardly mobile crowd of parvenus. Yet *The Life* also records Hardy's resentment of class distinctions. The internal conflict caused by his dramatic change in station is evident on every page: in the omissions and evasions, in the lack of structure and awkward juxtapositions, and in the degree of self-alienation implied in the maneuver of ghosting an autobiography in order to create a persona whose passivity is a clue to the problematic nature of ambition for Hardy.

*   *   *

An instance of Hardy's "edgewise" insertions which reveal so much "concealed beneath ambiguous expressions" is the following diary entry for April 28, 1888, included in *The Life*.

> "A short story of a young man—who could not go to Oxford—His struggles and ultimate failure. Suicide. [Probably the germ of *Jude the Obscure*.] There is something [in this] the world ought to be shown, and I am the one to show it to them—though I was not altogether hindered going, at least to Cambridge, and could have gone up easily at five-and-twenty." (LWTH, 216)

"A young man who could not go to Oxford"—we shall see in a moment how aptly the description fits the young Hardy. The entry implicitly asserts a connection between life and art: one writes about one's experience because it seems important and because it may be hidden from others. Hardy insists not only on the social importance of this story ("there is something in this the world ought to be shown") but also on his particular connection ("and I am the one to show it").

After the novel was published, Hardy consistently maintained that "no book he had ever written contained less of his own life"; he wrote an inquirer that "there is not a scrap of personal detail in [*Jude*], it having the least to do with his own life of all his books" (LWTH, 289, 425). He insisted that he intended

> to use the difficulty of a poor man's acquiring learning... merely as the "tragic mischief" (among others) of a dramatic story, for which purpose an old-fashioned university at the very door of the poor man was the most striking method.... *It is hardly necessary to add that he had no feeling in the matter,* and used Jude's difficulties of study as he would have used war, fire, or shipwreck for bringing about a catastrophe. (LWTH, 295–96, emphasis added)

The note of Olympian distance, of personal noninvolvement and artistic disengagement with his material, all are belied by the diary entry which Hardy included in *The Life* along with the above assertions.

It is characteristic that in the "germ," even before he makes his identification with the young man's experience explicit, Hardy begins to distance himself. To paraphrase both what is said and omitted: "I am the one to write this story because I shared this experience though I did not altogether share it." The impulse to be deeply involved in this projected fiction is immediately countered by the impulse to dissociate himself from his character. The "germ" reveals Hardy's understandable reluctance to expose his own situation to the public, even while implying that he was conscious of some experience of injustice which he shared and felt needed to be exposed.

What was Hardy's connection with the "story of a young man who could not go to Oxford"? Both recent biographers suggest that Hardy nursed until his mid-twenties the idea of going up to university and entering the Church. Apprenticeship to a local architect was a sensible, practical way for the son of a mason to begin the process of moving upward, but for Hardy it lacked the charisma of other avenues. He describes himself in *The Life* as "a born bookworm [who] had sometimes too wished to enter the Church. . . . at sixteen, though he had just begun to be interested in French and the Latin classics, the question arose of a profession or business" (LWTH, 31). He notes his disappointment when his scholarly friend Horace Moule did not encourage him to continue his classical studies, but he felt bound "to listen to reason and prudence" (LWTH, 38). Throughout his apprenticeship and years as an architect's clerk, Hardy maintained a substantial program of self-education, perhaps with an eye to late entry in university. But the apprenticeship was, in effect, all that his family could "do" for Hardy, and though he asserts in "the germ" that he could have gone up to Cambridge at twenty-five, it is highly unlikely that his father could have afforded the fees or that he could have won one of the few, highly competitive fellowships which went by and large to the sons of the well-to-do middle class. Not until the summer of 1866 does he seem to have abandoned the "visionary" scheme of a clerical career, giving intellectual doubts about doctrine as his reason in *The Life* (LWTH, 53); both biographers suggest that whatever the state of his conscience, the dream fell through ultimately because it wasn't economically feasible.

An oral tradition has it that in his late teens or early twenties, Hardy applied to the Theological Seminary at Salisbury with the thought of entering the Church as a licentiate and was rejected because of his social class or his lack of formal education. Though the concrete evidence for Hardy's application has not yet been produced, J. O. Bailey believes that such an attempt "seem[s to be] the basis for Jude's letter to the heads of the colleges at Christminster, and the snobbish reply from T. Tetuphenay." If Hardy did experience such a rejection, whether it was haughty in tone or merely seemed so to him, it would help to explain some of his bitter remarks about the clergy in his fiction.[9]

What lends the legend more credibility when taken in conjunction with his last novel is the short story which was the first fruit of the "germ" of *Jude the Obscure*. "A Tragedy of Two Ambitions" was sent off in August, 1888, four months after the diary entry. In this story the two brothers Halborough are prevented from going to Oxford because their father drinks up all the money their dead mother had put by for their university education. Instead they become first schoolmasters and then seminary students at Salisbury. The elder brother, Joshua, is bitter, ambitious, and class-conscious, galled that as licentiates he and his brother can "preach the Gospel—true ... but we can't rise!"[10] He reacts like Godwin Peak when his disreputable father shows up inopportunely at the college. The younger brother, who adumbrates Jude, is the passive, unconfident character who turns up frequently in Hardy's fiction. Together they epitomize the alternative directions in which an aspiring, sensitive poor man might move: diffident retreat or calculating advance.

Just when the careers of the brothers seem to be on the upswing, the father returns from Canada, threatening to blight their prospects once again. When they meet him by chance on a deserted road, he is so drunk that he stumbles into a weir and, thinking that this may be their salvation, the elder son hesitates to save him until it is too late. Their careers flourish, but at the story's end, both brothers regret that they have entered the Church, and each confesses that he has thought of suicide.

Here again is the theme of ambition which leads to betrayal. It is clear that Joshua Halborough is using the Church as a way to rise and that he is willing to make certain intellectual compromises to do so, although he tries to hide these from himself.

> "There's a fine work for any man of energy in the Church ..." he said fervidly. "Torrents of infidelity to be stemmed, new views of old subjects to be expounded, truths in spirit to be substituted for truths in the letter...." He lapsed into reverie with the vision of his career, persuading himself that it was ardour for Christianity which spurred him on, and not pride of place....
>
> "If the Church is elastic, and stretches to the shape of the time, she'll last, I suppose...."
> (89)

The distinction between "truths in spirit" and "truths in the letter" is reiterated in the epigraph to *Jude*, "The letter killeth"; another passage in the short story is interpolated in the novel, although the element of social ambition is much less conspicuous in *Jude*.

> "I am just now going right through Pusey's *Library of the Fathers*."
> "You'll be a bishop, Joshua, before you have done!"

> "Ah!" said the other bitterly, shaking his head. "Perhaps I might have been—I might have been! But where is my D.D. or LL.D.; and how be a bishop without that kind of appendage?...To hail Oxford or Cambridge as *alma mater* is not for me...." (90)

Compare this with the following passage in which Jude considers his future, congratulating himself on all the reading he had done on his own.

> "I know something of the Fathers, and something of Roman and English history.
>
>   "These things are only a beginning.... Hence I must next concentrate all my energies on settling in Christminster.... I'll be D.D. before I have done!... I can work hard. I have staying power in abundance.... Yes, Christminster shall be my Alma Mater...." (57)

Joshua Halborough justifies his concern about class in this way:

> "For a successful painter, sculptor, musician, author, who takes society by storm it is no drawback, it is sometimes even a romantic recommendation, to hail from outcasts and profligates. But for a clergyman of the Church of England!...it is fatal! To succeed in the Church, people must believe in you, first of all, as a gentleman, secondly as a man of means, thirdly as a scholar, fourthly as a preacher, fifthly, perhaps as a Christian,—but always first as a gentleman...." (93)

"A Tragedy of Two Ambitions" is more than an attack on the social and intellectual hypocrisy within the Church. It is, as Gissing said of Peak, "a study of a savagely aristocratic temperament," and possibly a frightening caricature of what Hardy felt he might have been. While we disapprove of Halborough's response to the temptations and pressure created by the class structure, we empathize, as we do in Gissing, with the cultural oppression and resentment felt by "a poor man who could not go to Oxford." If there had been some stinging experience of rejection in Hardy's past, it is not surprising (if we hold the example of Gissing in mind) that he so internalized his resentment that even two decades later his first treatment produced a story about the dangers of ambition. Class-consciousness and resentment here are character flaws in the upwardly mobile poor man, flaws for which he must be duly punished. By contrast Jude is an innocent, a "simpleton,"[11] whose class-consciousness is far more muted. He has none of Halborough's snobbery or ruthlessness, yet his very passivity seems to invite calamity. Together the story and novel show a protagonist caught in the no-win situation of the late-nineteenth century when a poor man was destined to feel compromised or betrayed by his ambition.

Whether or not Hardy ever applied to Salisbury Theological College, we know that from an early age he dreamed of a career in the Church, a career which was closed to him, finally, because of his class. Although Hardy makes light of his disappointment in *The Life,* other material indicates that he felt keenly the frustrated ambitions of his youth. As the initial impulse of the "germ" suggests, Hardy had a good deal in common with "a young man who could not go to Oxford" and felt that he was uniquely positioned to tell his story.

It is interesting that Hardy, like George Eliot, could not use in his fiction the positive solution he had discovered in his own life for the dilemma of an unclassed man. Writing was an admirable avenue for his talents, one that circumvented class barriers such as the education system and the social requirement that one be a "gentleman." But "the iron had entered his soul," as he often said, in the initial frustration of aspiration: this was the story he had to tell.

Far from "having the least to do with his life of all his books," *Jude the Obscure* is a return to Hardy's familial and personal past. Character and place names, particularly in the holograph version,[12] indicate that Hardy connected Jude's story with his paternal grandmother, Mary Head Hardy, whose memories of her childhood in Fawley, Berkshire, "were so poignant that she never cared to return to the place after she had left it as a young girl" (LWTH, 453). Hardy visited the village in 1892 when he was at work on *Jude,* noting: "Entered a ploughed vale which might be called the Valley of Brown Melancholy. The silence is remarkable.... Though I am alive with the living I can only see the dead here, and am scarcely conscious of the happy children at play" (LWTH, 265). Mary Head's story probably contributed a great deal to Tess, to Sue and Jude's unhappy family history, and to the theme of a family curse which would blight a marriage between cousins. Another family member is alluded to in the 1895 "Preface" to *Jude,* the woman whose death in 1890 suggested "some of the circumstances" of the novel. The reference is almost certainly to Hardy's cousin Tryphena Sparks, with whom Hardy had a close relationship, the precise nature of which we cannot know. Tryphena is one of the probable models for Sue. Jude is said to have been based "in part" on Hardy's uncle, Jack Antell, a self-taught cobbler, given to drink, who started a Latin school in Puddletown. Hardy composed the epitaph for his uncle's tombstone: "He was a man of considerable local reputation as a self-made scholar, having acquired a varied knowledge of languages, literature and science by unaided study, and in the face of many untoward circumstances."[13]

However, Jude's temperament, aspiration, and even his work as a restorer of church masonry connect him most closely with Hardy. The following passage from the novel is based on an incident described in *The Life* and quoted herein on page 45.

> Jude went out, and, feeling more than ever his existence to be an undemanded one, he lay down upon his back on a heap of litter near the pig-sty.... He pulled his straw hat over his face, and peered through the interstices of the plaiting at the white brightness, vaguely

reflecting. Growing up brought responsibilities, he found. Events did not rhyme quite as he had thought. . . . As you got older, and felt yourself to be at the centre of your time, and not at a point in its circumference, as you had felt when you were little, you were seized with a sort of shuddering, he perceived. All around you there seemed to be something glaring, garish, rattling, and the noises and glares hit upon the little cell called your life, and shook it, and warped it. If he could only prevent himself growing up! He did not want to be a man. (37–38)

While other passages in *The Life* do not afford the striking parallel of these straw hat scenes, they do further indicate the degree to which Jude is a portrait of the artist as a young boy.[14] Jude shares Hardy's passion for books, and his reading follows Hardy's, down to the Griesbach edition of The New Testament and the identical list of favorite passages in *The Iliad*. His literary allusions reflect Hardy's taste and scope, and bits of Hardy's poems are interpolated into the novel along with other reflections and experiences recorded in *The Life*. One of the most suggestive indications of Hardy's autobiographical involvement with Jude is his use of a quotation from Swinburne as the epigraph for Book II, when Jude goes to Christminster: "Save his own soul he hath no star." In *The Life* Hardy uses this phrase to describe his experience in his twenties as "an isolated student cast upon the billows of London with no protection but his brains—the young man of whom it may be said more truly than perhaps of any, that 'save his own soul he hath no star'" (LWTH, 58).

Hardy's poem "In the Seventies," a companion piece to the novel, indicates the intensity and strain of those youthful aspirations which he shared with Jude. It begins with a quotation from Job, a text from which Jude quotes frequently: *"Qui deridetur ab amico suo sicut ego"* (I am as one mocked of his neighbor).

> In the seventies I was bearing in my breast,
> > Penned tight,
> Certain starry thoughts that threw a magic light
> On the worktimes and the soundless hours of rest
> In the seventies; aye, I bore them in my breast
> > Penned tight.

Jude also cherishes a dream which throws "a magic light" around his work, a dream symbolized by Christminster, which appears on his horizon as a celestial city surrounded by a halo of light. In the second stanza of "In the Seventies," the poet's neighbors shake their heads and say, "Alas, / For his onward years and name unless he mend!" much as the inhabitants of Marygreen do at Jude's inglorious return.

> "You've j'ined a College by this time, I suppose?"
> "Ah, no!" said Jude. "I am almost as far off that as ever."
> "How so?"
> Jude slapped his pocket.

"Just what we thought! Such places be not for such as you—only for them with plenty o' money."

"There you are wrong," said Jude, with some bitterness. "They are for such ones!" (132)

In the poem the speaker's "vision" makes him immune to "the chillings of misprision / And the damps that choked my goings to and fro."

> In the seventies nought could darken or destroy it,
> Locked in me,
> Though as delicate as lamp-worm's lucency;
> Neither mist nor murk could weaken or alloy it
> In the seventies!—could not darken or destroy it,
> Locked in me.

Although the "vision" is unforgettable, perhaps even indestructible, the poem suggests a coming disillusionment which is realized in the novel when Jude is obliged to subject his dream of Christminster to reality. After his townsmen's disparaging remarks, he abandons "the imaginative world" in which his success is assured and thinks of "practicabilities"; he sends off his letters of inquiry to the college heads with crushing results.

Jude is drawn from Hardy's childhood and young manhood, and it sketches an alternative outcome to a young man's dream of self-development. The "germ" of the novel lay in Hardy's disappointment in not going to university, in his experiences of frustration and perhaps of rejection, in his groping for a way to realize himself, and in his fear that his talents, like Jude's, might be wasted. However, the experience of desolation, for which Jude is justly famous, does not derive entirely from a realistic presentation of the difficulties which beset an aspiring poor man in a particular historical period. It is also a reflection of the desolation of Hardy's soul as he pondered the discontinuity between past and present, feeling socially and intellectually uprooted in both Dorset and London. While Jude is in one sense "the simple self," uncompromised yet nonetheless destroyed by his dreams, he is also the mature Hardy, whose inner "tragedy of unfulfilled aims" Jude enacts. The "vision" and aspirations which Hardy cherished as a young man gave way to the darkness of the "In Tenebris" poems, which have as epigraphs quotations from the Psalms worthy of Jude's final days. In these poems and in "The Dead Man Walking," also written in 1896, Hardy, like Jude, expresses suicidal longings. The conclusion of "In Tenebris I" would make an equally suitable epitaph for author or character.

> Black is night's cope;
> But death will not appal
> One who, past doubtings all,
> Waits in unhope.

Far from being occasioned by the public reaction to his last novel, these poems are the fruit of the same experience that produced the fiction. As I suggested earlier, Hardy's philosophical pessimism is grounded in the double bind situation of an ambitious poor man for whom either success or failure means alienation. *Jude the Obscure* supplies the connection between social experience and world view.

*   *   *

In the 1895 "Preface" to *Jude,* Hardy wrote that his novel dealt with "the fret and fever, derision and disaster, that may press in the wake of the strongest passion known to humanity: to tell, without a mincing of words, of a deadly war waged between flesh and spirit; and to point the tragedy of unfulfilled aims...." From the first, near-hysterical responses to "Jude the Obscene," critics have focussed on Jude's sexuality as if it—or love—were unquestionably "the strongest passion known to humanity," and as if the height of his unfulfillment were his frustrations with Sue. Immediately after publication, Hardy wrote Edmund Gosse to correct the emphasis in his friend's early review, asserting that his novel "is concerned first with the labours of a poor student to get a University degree" (LWTH, 513), and we have seen that the "germ" for *Jude* was such a story. Jude's "strongest passion" is to realize himself, to be free to develop. Christminster is a principal means to this end, the only arena in which Jude can imagine himself being fulfilled. The "deadly war waged between flesh and spirit" is at least as much a matter of those objective limitations which prevent a man from realizing his aspirations as it is of being tempted by sex.

However, it is clear that a variety of factors contribute to Jude's "tragedy of unfulfilled aims." There are his character flaws: his appetite for sex and drink which, combined with his passive, feckless nature, contribute to an impression that Jude is self-destructive. Then, too, Jude is "a tragic Don Quixote" (226), a romantic idealist destined for disillusionment and despair. There are external hindrances to his development: his poverty and lack of schooling; the narrow provincial world; marriage laws and conventional morality; the callousness of those within the university; the pettiness of those without; the continual pressure of "the mean bread-and-cheese question" (103). Finally there are extra-societal factors—a family curse, the Zeitgeist, the "coming universal wish not to live," Darwinian nature in which man is trapped like a rabbit in a gin. The multiplicity of causes suggests that Hardy was uncertain about the nature of the tragedy he wished to write, and in attempting to portray Jude's situation as representative of the human condition, he greatly expanded the social basis of Jude's tragedy. At the root of his original conception, however, is the crucial fact that Jude is an aspiring poor man whose character is shaped partly in response to the class structure.

The chapters on Jude's rejection from Christminster demonstrate Hardy's insight into the psychological damage which the class system does to a poor man. Here he shows how social factors are internalized as individual guilt. After years of arduous, lonely self-study, years spent dreaming of Christminster as "the heavenly Jerusalem," the antithesis of the "meanly utilitarian" world of Marygreen, Jude arrives in the city. Dreamer that he is, he lacks any clear plan for entering the university, hoping that his mere presence in the town will effect some change. His muddling indirection as he approaches Christminster probably mirrors Hardy's youthful diffidence and uncertainty, and Hardy seems at times to fault his character on this account. Jude is ineffectual, but there is not a great deal that he can do to further his situation. He builds universities in the air because there is no real way to enter the earthly ones. In the past the universities had been open to "such ones" as Jude, as he asserts, but during the mid-nineteenth century they were essentially closed to the poor. Sue is hyperbolic but not altogether unfair in saying that Jude is "elbowed off the pavements by the millionaires' sons" (171).[15]

Jude's situation is aggravated by the contradiction between the reality—a class structure using the educational system to maintain and reinforce class differences—and the ideology which authorizes upward mobility and which claimed liberal education as a classless value. Apologists for the Idea of the University—men like Arnold, Newman, Jowett, and Pattison—helped to legitimate the authority of educational institutions, thus confirming their role in defining a privileged elite. Jude takes his idea of Christminster straight out of Matthew Arnold, whom he quotes on his first night in the town. "Beautiful city, so venerable, so lovely, so unravaged by the fierce intellectual life of our century, so serene. . . . Her ineffable charm keeps ever calling us to the true goal of all of us, to the ideal, to perfection" (100). Jude wholeheartedly accepts the authority of the university, and its power over his imagination is evident in his night vision of Christminster when he communes with the ghosts of Gibbon, Peel, Pusey, Keble, and Wesley—all men of Christminster, all men with whom he identifies. His ambition is to enlarge his horizons by studying "the best that has been thought and said." But to pursue this classless ideal of Arnold's, this spiritualized version of upward mobility, Jude must gain entrance to an institution from which he is excluded specifically because of his class. He is betrayed not by his lust or his gluttony but by the class structure of his society, a structure deeply entrenched and on the defensive, using education as a way of maintaining a social hierarchy.

The irony of celebrating a university because it has been unravaged by intellectual life is lost on Jude, who also fails to recall, when he is quoting Arnold, that Oxford is "the home of lost causes." His name, of course, links him to the patron saint of lost causes. The ironies suggest both that Jude belongs at Christminster and that as a persistent idealist, he cannot see the university clearly nor grasp that it will be the site of his failure and not his triumph. Yet in spite of these ironies, the chapter remains a moving evocation of Christminster; we see her much as Jude does, much as Arnold and Newman and, one suspects, Hardy saw Oxford.

Jude's perspective on his situation is deeply confused. Condemning himself for past weaknesses, Jude is nevertheless convinced that he belongs at Christminster. Criticizing his failure to get information and to lay solid plans, he still hesitates to act and avoids a face-to-face encounter with one of the college masters. Instead he writes to five of them.

> When the letters were posted Jude mentally began to criticize them; he wished they had not been sent. "It is just one of those intrusive, vulgar, pushing, applications which are so common in these days," he thought. "Why couldn't I know better than address utter strangers in such a way? I may be an imposter, an idle scamp, a man with a bad character, for all that they know to the contrary. . . . Perhaps that's what I am!" (134)

Jude's confidence in the appropriateness of his ambition is undermined. He had thought that his desire to surpass the limitations on his development—to get out of Marygreen—was ennobling, a way of becoming his "best self"; but once expressed, even modestly, his desire appears to him "intrusive, vulgar, pushing." Identifying with the men in the ivory tower, he unthinkingly adopts their condescension; seeing his action through their eyes, he condemns it. Because his application to the university is one of many from men as poor as he, Jude imagines that it is therefore "common," that is to say, ignoble. Overwhelmed by this self-doubt, he ends by convincing himself that he is actually unworthy of admission: "I may be an imposter. . . . Perhaps that's what I am!" In fact he is an imposter of sorts at this moment, for he is a poor man thinking like a privileged man, and so denying the truth of his own experience. In taking up the values of an elite—values which seem to him to be noble—he fails to realize at this point how those values are made to work against him.

Only one of the five college heads answers Jude's letter. Tetuphenay of Biblioll College writes:

> Sir—I have read your letter with interest; and, judging from your description of yourself as a working-man, I venture to think that you will have a much better chance of success in life by remaining in your own sphere and sticking to your trade than by adopting any other course. That, therefore, is what I advise you to do. Yours faithfully. . . . (136)

At first Jude's sense of justice is outraged, and in anger he chalks a quotation from Job on the wall of the college: "I have understanding as well as you; I am not inferior to you: yea, who knoweth not such things as these?" But by the next morning, "he laughed at his self-conceit." Rereading the letter, he is struck by the "wisdom" in its lines and sees "himself as a fool indeed." Rather than protesting, Jude accepts Tetuphenay's judgment on his dream.

Why should Jude's anger turn inward to self-denigration? Is he a quitter, given too easily to despair? One whose desires pathetically exceed his talents? Is Christminster an unreasonable dream? Is Tetuphenay's advice really "sensible"? Jude's contradictory reaction to his own and to Tetuphenay's letters dramatizes how a social inferior comes to terms with what he perceives to be legitimate authority. Hardy is unsparing in showing the high personal cost of this accommodation. The authority which Jude invests in Christminster he steals from himself, so that he has no self-respect when Christminster denies him. After his initial anger, Jude accepts complete personal responsibility for his failure, believing that what happened *ought* to have happened and that his rejection is the appropriate response of the world to the inadequacy of Jude Fawley.[16]

Nor are the consequences of this accommodation purely personal. Jude's contempt for himself extends to his fellow working-men. In the heat of his initial anger at Tetuphenay's letter, he turns back to the working community, with whom he has been permanently lumped, and sees "that the town life was a book of humanity infinitely more palpitating, varied, and compendious than the gown life. These struggling men and women before him were the reality of Christminster, though they knew little of Christ or Minster. . . . He had tapped the real Christminster life" (137). But by the next morning when he sees himself through the eyes of those in power as "a fool indeed," he equally sees his fellow men as degraded, drunken, and ignorant. He seeks out a disreputable tavern and there uses his learning as a weapon against the community to prove his superiority. On a bet, to prove an empty boast, he drunkenly recites the creed in Latin, and then exclaims:

> "You pack of fools! . . . Which of you knows whether I have said it or no? It might have been the Rat-catcher's Daughter in double Dutch for all that your besotted heads can tell! See what I have brought myself to—the crew I have come among!" (142)

By accepting Tetuphenay's judgment, Jude becomes "convinced that he was at bottom a vicious character, of whom it was hopeless to expect anything"; consequently he acts that way and judges his fellow men equally negatively.

Jude's self-destructive failures of will and appetite are related to his consciousness of his inferior position in a hierarchical society and to the impotence he experiences in trying to better himself. His idealism, too, is a response to his deprivation. Even as a youth, "his dreams were as gigantic as his surroundings were small" (41).[17] In her study of Hardy's fiction, Jean Brooks writes that *Jude the Obscure* "probes the existentialist's terrible freedom and the burden of unlocalized guilt; in the search for self-definition, self-knowledge, self-sufficiency [Hardy embodies] the impulse to self-destruction, long before Freud, as self-punishment for the guilt of aspiring personal being." Albert Guerard took a similar line more than two decades ago in his psychological study of Hardy.[18] Both critics suggest that Jude's psychological situation is typical of "modern" or "existential" man, but as we have seen, there are specific historical factors which shape Jude's character. What he feels as "unlocalized guilt" is a consequence of the clash between his middle-class aspirations and his working-class status; his self-punishment for "aspiring personal being" is the sort of internal control the system needs to preserve the status quo. Part of Hardy's greatness is that he could use the class structure and the prosaic experience of mobility to evoke central issues about human nature and destiny. When Hardy universalizes his characters, placing them in the context of tragic heroes of Western literature, he does so because he can see arising from their ordinary experience those conflicts and high emotions which we associate with tragedy. A sociological interpretation of Hardy's work should not reduce it to historical chronicle but place appropriate emphasis on the materials he used: Hardy saw tragedy where others see only the most commonplace of experiences. It's only right that we appreciate the particulars of that commonplace experience in order to see what Hardy has made of it.

*   *   *

In Jude's continuing effort to come to terms with his ambition, we feel that "discord of approval and anxiety" about social change to which Irving Howe referred. Indeed, Hardy could present Jude's self-doubt so admirably because he had shared so much of it. Like Jude, he questioned his motives ("A Tragedy of Two Ambitions" suggests how far he could go in imaginatively probing the combination of ambition and resentment of the class structure). Like Jude, he saw danger in the social transformation produced by widespread social mobility and felt an anxious concern to distinguish between his own aspirations and those of "vulgar, pushing" men. The following is a diary entry from 1891, made when Hardy was preparing material for Jude and had returned from a visit to the British Museum.

> "Crowds parading and gaily traipsing round the mummies, thinking to-day is for ever, and the girls casting sly glances at young men across the swathed dust of Mycerinus[?] They pass with flippant comments the illuminated MSS.—the labours of years—and stand under Rameses the Great, joking. Democratic government may be justice to man, but it will probably merge in proletarian, and when these people are our masters it will lead to more of this contempt, and possibly be the utter ruin of art and literature!" (LWTH, 247)

That Hardy's resentment of the injustices of the class structure existed side by side with such anti-democratic sentiments contributes to our difficulty in understanding the narrator's attitude toward Jude and Christminster. Is Jude a "tragic Don Quixote" or a feckless youth whose academic ambitions are easily sidetracked by Arabella's provocative missile? Are his ambitions foolish, or is

Christminster wrong to reject him? Is there any intellectual life within the colleges, or are they merely rotting buildings supported by laborers such as Jude? How do we respond to that purportedly classless, ghost-filled world which Jude greets on his first night? The narrator's assessment of Jude and his dream seems to be inconsistent.

When we come to a passage in *Jude* like the one below, it is difficult to know what to make of it. Is this part of Jude's self-destructive failure of confidence or is it genuine soul-searching, a discovery of ignoble motives that had fueled his dream of entering the university? The passage captures the double bind situation in which, I argue, Hardy as well as his character found himself.

> The old fancy which had led on to the culminating vision of the bishopric had not been an ethical or theological enthusiasm at all, but a mundane ambition masquerading in a surplice. He feared that his whole scheme had degenerated to, even though it might not have originated in, a social unrest which had no foundation in the nobler instincts; which was purely an artificial product of civilization. There were thousands of young men on the same self-seeking track at the present moment. The sensual hind who ate, drank, and lived carelessly with his wife through the days of his vanity was a more likeable being than he. (148)

There are no viable options in Jude's analysis; he is either on a "self-seeking track" with "thousands" of others, or he remains a "sensual hind" who sticks to his "sphere" and finds the ordinary amount of physical satisfactions. Full of self-loathing, Jude determines to turn his back on his dreams and ambitions, punishing himself in a way but also searching for alternative paths toward self-fulfillment.

In Books III, IV, and V Hardy explores through his character the possibility of denying ambition and shunning what the narrator calls "the modern vice of unrest." Are there as yet unexplored chances for a poor man to realize himself "in his own sphere"? Characteristically in a Bildungsroman the defeated, idealistic youth accepts reality and seeks some compromise with a social order which has fallen far short of his dreams. Jude now explores this possibility of compromise.

He first chooses the "purgatorial course" of becoming a licentiate, but his intellectual convictions and emotions combine to make this career an impossibility too. He then renounces any spiritual vocation, resolving to live a decent, ordinary life, turning to manual labor as a "sphere" as vital as any other. With Sue he learns that the working community is small-minded and conventionally self-righteous, and that modern labor is not likely to foster that "palpitating, varied, [or] compendious life" Jude had briefly imagined among the townspeople of Christminster.

As a mason in church restoration, Jude's work connects him to a "dead" world from which he is now intellectually alienated. Sue urges him to "fall back upon railway stations, bridges, theatres, music-halls, hotels—everything that has no connection with conduct" (325), hoping thus to win a measure of independence by divorcing their private and public lives. What she thinks of as neutral buildings without symbolic significance express values of the modern world: the freedom of a rootlessness and transiency suggested by trains and hotels, the dominance of the city, the spread of urban culture in which autonomy is gained at the expense of community. The structures Sue mentions are all public places which contribute to "the modern vice of unrest"—places where individuals mass together without forming genuine relationships, coming there to be sheltered alone, or moved, or entertained before they depart. Working on buildings to which he is connected in no meaningful way, the modern mason creates a world for people without connections. Changing times force Jude out of the past, out of the stoneyard, but the present affords him no satisfying world.

For several years Sue and Jude lead "a shifting, almost nomadic, life" (328), Jude doing stonecutting for town halls, museums, or hotels until he falls ill and turns to marketing gingerbread at fairs near railway stations. His "Christminster cakes," a mockery of the dreams he had as a baker's apprentice, are nevertheless evidence of his unquenched passion for some worthier labor. "Still harping on Christminster—even in his cakes!" laugh[s] Arabella. "Just like Jude. A ruling passion" (331). Although Sue tells her, "We gave up all ambition, and were never so happy in our lives till his illness came," Arabella is shrewd in her observation about Jude's "ruling passion." He falls sick from the wandering, sick from his failure to realize himself in productive work. The barrenness of the laboring world, even with Sue and his children, brings Jude back to "Christminster Again" with a gnawing sense of the injustice done him. "I can't help it. I love the place—although it hates all men like me, the so-called self-taught" (340).

The climax of the "story of a young man who could not go to Oxford" and the high-water mark of Jude's understanding of his situation is his speech to the townspeople on Remembrance Day, in which he protests the right of all men and women to dream, to challenge the social order rather than accepting the status quo, to develop themselves beyond the limits of the "spheres" into which they are born. The setting recalls his drunken evening in a Christminster tavern, some years earlier, when he had recited the creed of an alien institution in an alien tongue reserved for an elite which excluded him. Now instead of haranguing the townsfolk, he becomes their true pastor, offering a new creed out of his own experience and in language which they can understand. He stands among the crowd outside the Sheldonian, waiting to see an academic procession. Offering to translate a Latin inscription in the stone, he finds "that the people all round him were listening with interest [so he goes on] to describe the carving of the frieze . . . and to criticize some details of masonry in other college fronts about the city" (344). Eventually he is recognized as "the tutor of St. Slums," and asked to give an account of himself.

> It is a difficult question, my friends, for any young man—that question I had to grapple with, and which thousands are weighing at the present moment in these uprising times—whether to follow uncritically the track he finds himself in, without considering his aptness for it, or to consider what his aptness or bent may be, and re-shape his course accordingly. I tried to do the latter, and I failed. But I don't admit that my failure proved my view to be a wrong one, or that my success would have made it a right one; though that's how we appraise such attempts nowadays—I mean, not by their essential soundness, but by their accidental outcomes.... (345)

Throughout this scene Jude remains psychologically convincing, a man reflecting on his fortunes and on what experience has taught him, not an ideologue with a certain answer. However, his thrust is clear: success in his society is no fair measure of the worth of a man. His struggle to raise himself from his station was appropriate and honorable. If his "impulses—affections— vices perhaps they should be called" have hampered him, it is only because a man must be "as cold-blooded as a fish and as selfish as a pig to have a really good chance of being one of his country's worthies" (345). Success is won at too great a cost to the whole man. As for his failure, he asserts that "it was my poverty and not my will that consented to be beaten. It takes two or three generations to do what I tried to do in one." That is Jude's clearest insight that the problem is outside himself in the socio-economic structure.

After a despairing aside, he continues:

> And what I appear, a sick and poor man, is not the worst of me. I am in a chaos of principles—groping in the dark—acting by instinct and not after example. Eight or nine years ago when I came here first, I had a neat stock of fixed opinions, but they dropped away one by one; and the further I get the less sure I am. I doubt if I have anything for my present rule of life than following inclinations which do me and nobody else any harm, and actually give pleasure to those I love best.... I cannot explain further here. I perceive there is something wrong somewhere in our social formulas: what it is can only be discovered by men or women with greater insight than mine,—if, indeed, they ever discover it—at least in our time. "For who knoweth what is good for man in this life?—and who can tell a man what shall be after him under the sun?"
>
> "Hear, hear," said the populace.
>
> "Well preached!" said Tinker Taylor.... "Why, one of them jobbing pa'sons swarming about here, that takes the services when our head Reverends want a holiday, wouldn't ha' discoursed such a doctrine for less than a guinea down?... And this only a working man!" (346)

Consider the effect the novel would have if Hardy had ended it with this chapter. Jude, a working man, stands with a child on his hip, his companion, not his wife, beside him, talking with other laborers, organizing their experience around new ideas rather than around outworn notions of social and moral order, protesting the "social formulas" which hampered him and which are no longer appropriate, if, indeed, they ever were. It is, above all, a scene of working men, just outside the walls of academe, thinking independently. "As a sort of objective commentary" on Jude's remarks, an ascetic Doctor in black robes pulls up at the curb and hurries inside, his driver alighting to kick his horse in the belly.

> "If that can be done," said Jude, "at college gates in the most religious and educational city in the world, what shall we say as to how far we've got?"
>
> "Order!" said one of the policemen.... "Keep yer tongue quiet, my man, while the procession passes."

Fade out, with the agents of social order ominously present but no longer with any moral authority.

*   *   *

This is not, of course, our final impression. Book VI complicates our view of *Jude* as a social tragedy. The protagonist's defeat becomes private and mystified, and this is nowhere more obvious than in his death on Remembrance Day, which is emphatically counterpointed with his return to Christminster a year earlier. The image of Jude the artisan, talking earnestly with other men, publicly protesting "social formulas," is replaced with Jude isolated, ignored by all in his lonely room, his dying words interrupted periodically by the crude "Hurrahs!" of a crowd insensible of everything save its own pleasure. Any alliance with the people, any hope for corrective action, is impossible.

Between these two scenes intrude the incongruous murders and suicide of Father Time, which force the tragedy on to a metaphysical ground. In terms of "a short story of a young man who could not go to Oxford," the catastrophe is gratuitous and unrelated; one might argue than in a lurid, sensational touch, Christminster is shown to be a "killer," the literal destroyer of Jude's "unfulfilled aims," so dreadful does the city appear to little Father Time. But the allusions to Christminster as the Jerusalem of the crucifixion suggest that it is the setting for some timeless human tragedy, the slaughter of the innocents and the death of hope. As Norman Holland has suggested, Hardy offers a parody of that sacrifice through which hope was returned to the world and time redeemed; Time himself dangles ingloriously and dreadfully before our eyes.[19]

Throughout Book VI, even in Jude's address to the people of Christminster, the element of social protest is muted as the theme of cosmic injustice is developed. At the midpoint of his speech, just after Jude asserts the dignity of his ambition, comes the now-familiar counterthrust of doubt: "I may ... be a sort of success as a frightful example of what not to do.... I was, perhaps, after all, a paltry victim to the spirit of mental and social restlessness, that makes so many unhappy in these days!" One is reminded of the narrator's disapproval of "the modern vice of unrest." There is a "dying fall" in Jude's words, "something wrong somewhere in our social formulas: what it is can only be discovered by men or women with greater insight than mine,—if, indeed, they ever discover it. . . ." By "social formulas" Jude may mean the institution of marriage, the difficulty of divorce, the ideal of permanent conjugal love, the nuclear family (he favors bringing up children communally), the system of education, the condition of manual laborers, the idea of "spheres" or social classes, and so on. Hardy's indictment of these "social formulas" is so comprehensive that he dissipates any confidence in man's ability to change the social order. Earlier, Sue reflects that "the social moulds civilisation fits us into have no more relations to our actual shapes than the conventional shapes of the constellations have to the real star-patterns" (226). Sue is describing a permanent human condition, and her statement implies that these social "moulds" and "formulas" are inevitable curtailments of human potential.

In accounting for the catastrophe, Hardy harks back to his idea of a family curse on Sue and Jude, reminds us of Jude's "two Arch Enemies . . . [his] weakness for womankind, and [his] impulse to strong liquor" (373), and has Jude speculate about a "First Cause [that] worked automatically like a somnambulist, and not reflectively like a sage" (362), all of which tends to dispel the force of Jude's perception that it was his "poverty" and not his "will" which had shaped his life. Yet he remains strong against the temptation to blame himself for his disaster; his great growth is that he no longer internalizes the social conditions which have brought him to his knees, in clear contrast to Sue, who completely capitulates to the idea that the outward "success" of their lives reflects their worth or the rightness of their aims. In her intense, masochistic guilt, she flees back to the old law, back to the Church, back to Phillotson, wailing, "We must conform! . . . There is no choice. . . . It is no use fighting against God!" To which Jude responds to his bitter end: "It is only against man and senseless circumstance" (362). But to have Jude die quoting Job tends to put his tragedy in the context of a metaphysical mystery of evil rather than in the context of historical and potentially remediable social experience. When Jude dies, his own worth and his insights go for naught, and he is replaced by Arabella and Vilbert, who represent an amoral order which will continue to ignore human aspiration.

After Father Time's gruesome act, Jude is cut off from the townspeople and denied the typicality which might be associated with his obscurity. He is singled out as exceptional, a tragic protagonist who, despite his worthiness, is inevitably doomed to suffer. Why? we are bound to ask. Is it the commandments he has broken in living with Sue? the penalty for "aspiring personal being"? the folly of idealism? Jude's questioning of the moral order in his reference to "a chaos of darkness" appears to invoke the catastrophe, the breakdown of any order and sense in the murder of children by children.

In the Aldbrickham church where Sue and Jude worked, a warden tells of some painters who were restoring a church; after drinking all night with Satan, they fall asleep and awaken to find the Ten Commandments painted with the "nots" left out. It is as though without the "social formulas," the "nots," the prohibitions, mere anarchy would be loosed upon the world—or at least upon him who challenges the old order. The enormity of the disaster which Hardy heaps on Jude for what he calls alternately his "crime," "flaw," and "curse" may reflect Hardy's anxiety about the breakdown of social and intellectual structures. In the device of the grotesque child, Hardy implies that "Time" will not bring about the social change which Jude hopes for and urges the necessity of. The boy's act stops "Time" and obliterates the future in the murder of Jude's children (who might realize Jude's ambitions) and in his own acting out of the "coming universal wish not to live" (356).

*   *   *

Hardy could see the tragic potential in the "story of a young man who could not go to Oxford." He wished to tell that story, but he had other competing wishes too. His ambivalence about social change in general and about his own mobility in particular led him to obscure his challenge to the class structure and show Jude's career embodying man's fate in an unmeaning universe. In a diary entry from 1892, just after his visit to Great Fawley, Hardy noted, probably with *Jude* in mind: "The best tragedy—highest tragedy in short—is that of the WORTHY encompassed by the INEVITABLE" (LWTH, 265). While the discrepancy between Jude's aspirations and his social status is at the heart of his tragedy, Hardy chose to regard this discrepancy as part of the inevitable human condition rather than as an effect of a particular social organization. This was made all the easier in that his own outward success had seemed to bring him the same philosophical despair that Jude feels. Resentment of the class structure certainly informed his characterization and led him to explore tentatively alternatives to liberal ideology. Jude is drawn toward other working men and glimpses collective solutions to social problems. Those possibilities are undeniably cut off in the novel, but even raising them is exceedingly unusual in fiction of the period. Forced back on liberal ideology—that is, forced to see Jude as an individual isolated from other men by his fate—Hardy showed the hollowness of that ideology: the absurdity of the idea that man was free to realize himself. His novel is essentially an anti-Bildungsroman in which Jude's formation or education leads him to "a chaos of principles" and in which not even the most radical compromise of his aspiration permits an accommodation with the social order.

* * *

Hardy's consciousness that upward mobility had failed to bring him fulfillment increased through the years and found expression in his conviction that everyone's experience *un*teaches; wisdom comes only with painful loss. This conviction is embodied in Jude's contradictory development. Outwardly he moves consistently downhill, toward increasingly reduced material circumstances and an increasingly obscure social position. No matter how radically he reduces his ambition, he cannot obtain the most modest degree of contentment. At the same time, he grows in appreciating the complex nature of his desires and in understanding and correctly evaluating the world. He achieves the narrator's perspective that the world is not designed to satisfy the peculiarly human impulses and desires for justice, harmony, or self-development.

Hardy originally seems to have conceived of *Jude the Obscure* as a social tragedy in the naturalistic, or Zola-esque mode. Jude's flaws, his appetite for drink and sex and his lack of "staying power" (57), associate him with the type of lower-class man whose environment and heredity doom him to fail in realizing his finer ambitions. But Hardy also connected the plight of a particular class with the experience of intellectual and emotional disorientation so crucial to late-Victorians. He recognized, as Gissing had, that bourgeois culture, despite its attractions, was rotting from within—undermined by intellectual discoveries which made its world view untenable. Recognizing that Jude is born about two centuries too late for Christminster, Hardy makes his tragedy in some ways that of any nineteenth-century bourgeois intellectual for whom learning has been associated with painful loss of certainties. Calling Jude "a paltry victim [of] the spirit of *mental* and *social* restlessness, that makes so many unhappy in these days!" (345, emphasis added), he drops the issue of social mobility in Books III-V in order to develop the theme of intellectual alienation. Although Jude's outward career ceases to parallel Hardy's, his mental development continues to mirror his author's. In these books, Hardy's attention is divided between Sue and Jude as he explores their problematic freedom from sexual and social conventions. Here, then, is a second major theme of the novel, the theme so profitably discussed by David DeLaura and Robert Heilman as "the ache of modernism."[20] Engrossing as this aspect of the novel is, its connection to the story of Jude's social unrest is not fully articulated. By comparing Jude with Godwin Peak we can get a sense of what the connection is: both characters associate their self-development with entry into a culture that is already intellectually obsolescent; their "modern" spirit, as much as their social class, makes them unfit for the only society which appeals to their conservative imaginations, a society they continue to yearn for even as it damages their self-esteem, even as their resentment corrodes their dream of belonging. The "mental restlessness" that is the mark of their intellectual integrity is at cross-purposes with a "social restlessness" they can assuage, if at all, only by compromising their integrity.

It was the conflation of the disillusioned idealist with the Zola-esque protagonist—that is, the conflation of the stories of mental and social restlessness—which so angered the reading public in 1895. They had accepted Hardy's pessimism in the past, but they were outraged by the spectacle of a man of Jude's background and constitution arriving at the world view of this well-known, distinguished author. The intellectual challenges to Victorian society were far more unsettling when accompanied by a challenge to the social hierarchy. This "who does Jude think he is?" note was sounded most clearly by Edmund Gosse.

> ... it is not quite evident whether the claim on Jude's passions, or the inherent weakness of his inherited character, is the source of his failure. Perhaps both. But it is difficult to see what part Oxford has in his destruction, or how Mr. Hardy can excuse the rhetorical diatribes against the university which appear towards the close of the book. Does the novelist really think that it was the duty of the heads of houses to whom Jude wrote his crudely pathetic letters to offer him immediately a fellowship? [An interesting assumption, since Jude's letter is not given in the novel.] We may admit to the full pathos of Jude's position—nothing is more heart-rending than the obscurity of the half-educated—but surely the fault did not lie with Oxford.[21]

Gosse's condescension must have been the more shattering since in so many ways Hardy felt that he *was* Jude: that he had only by good fortune escaped sharing his social "obscurity," and that he even now shared with him a philosophical "obscurity" which was by no means "half-educated."

Clearly hurt by Gosse's and others' reactions to *Jude the Obscure* as "indecent" and "obscene," Hardy was cautious in his defense. In a letter to Gosse he stated that the "'grimy' features" to which his friend had objected were there

> to show the contrast between the ideal life a man wished to lead, and the squalid real life he was fated to lead. The throwing of the pizzle, at the supreme moment of his young dream, is to sharply initiate this contrast. . . . The idea was meant to run all through the novel. It is, in fact, to be discovered in *everybody's* life, though it lies less on the surface perhaps than it does in my poor puppet's. (LWTH, 514)

With friends like Gosse and reviewers like Jeannette Gilder who titled her article on *Jude* "Hardy the Degenerate," one can appreciate Hardy's concern to stress the universal quality of the tragedy and his eagerness to conceal the autobiographical elements in his novel. Gosse's review doubtless ensured

Hardy's later insistence that Jude's failure to go to university was merely part of the "tragic machinery" or "tragic mischief" and that "he had no feeling in the matter." Near the end of his life, when he was far removed from the preoccupations of his young manhood, there was talk of dramatizing *Jude,* and Hardy wrote:

> Would not Arabella be the villain of the piece?—or Jude's personal constitution?—so far as there is any villain more than blind Chance. Christminster is of course the tragic influence on Jude's drama in one sense, but innocently so, and merely as crass obstruction. By the way it is not meant to be exclusively Oxford, but any old-fashioned University about the date of the story, 1860–1870, before there were such chances for poor men as there are now. I have somewhere printed that I had no feeling against Oxford in particular. (LWTH, 467)

"Well, time cures hearts of tenderness" and bitterness, too, which is, perhaps, as well—for those of us who are comfortably circumstanced.[22]

We have seen that the "germ" of *Jude the Obscure* lay in Hardy's uneasy identification with "a poor man who could not go to Oxford"—and it is worth noting again that it is Hardy himself, disguised as his own biographer, who tells us that. We have seen, too, that the issue of Jude's social class does not remain the central focus of the "tragedy of unfulfilled aims," and that Jude's class-consciousness is expanded and then dissolved in a tragic consciousness of cosmic injustice. We have seen that Hardy vigorously denied any connections between himself and his character, and in later life, assuming an Olympian detachment, spoke of Christminster as an innocent "tragic influence," indicating that "the villain of the piece" would be first Arabella, then Jude's character, then "blind Chance." It seems that the original impetus to write *Jude* had to be censored and rechannelled in the terms of a universal tragedy which masked the social implications before Hardy found it acceptable to present to his middle-class public. Even then that public took offense in his connection of the stories of "mental and social restlessness." Hardy was uneasy about his identification with his unclassed characters and conscious of ambivalent intentions in writing novels which forced him to review and examine his experience of deracination. After *Jude,* his most searching assessment of "the simple self that was," he gave up novel-writing altogether and turned to lyric poetry as a more congenial literary form.

Though he was always careful about his public image, I think he must have derived satisfaction from the fact that the "dark horse" from below had challenged the middle-class conviction that certain "artificial forms," among them the class structure, were "cardinal facts of life." A month after *Jude the Obscure* was published, Hardy noted in his diary "a remark on one or two of the reviews."

Tragedy may be created by an opposing environment either of things inherent in the universe, or of human institutions. If the former be the means exhibited and deplored, the writer is regarded as impious; if the latter, as subversive and dangerous; when all the while he may never have questioned the necessity or urged the non-necessity of either.... (LWTH, 290)

The remark is so characteristic of others in *The Life,* couched in the third person, formal, and ultimately evasive: he *may* never have questioned, but then again, he may have; he leaves the door open. After all, he had written the novel, and noted just after it was finished: "Never retract. Never explain. Get it done and let them howl."

Figure 3. Arnold Bennett
(Courtesy of the National Portrait Gallery, London)

Bennett: Celebrating the Ordinary

*Here was a class [writers] that seemed to bridge the gulf. On the
one hand essentially Low, but by factitious circumstances
capable of entering upon those levels of social superiority to
which all true English aspire, those levels from which one may
tip a butler, scorn a tailor, and even commune with those who
lead "men" into battle. "Almost like gentlefolks"—that was it!*

H. G. Wells, Kipps (1905)

*I do not belong to [the middle class] by birth. Artists very seldom
do. I was born slightly beneath it. But by the help of God and
strict attention to business I have gained the right of entrance
into it. I admit that I have imitated its deportment, with certain
modifications of my own; I think its deportment is in many
respects worthy of imitation.... But the philosopher in me
cannot... melt away my profound and instinctive hostility to
this class.*

Arnold Bennett, "Middle Class" (1909)

Bennett may seem an unlikely figure to include in a study of the double bind of
upward mobility, for few writers have embraced success more enthusiastically.
He was born in Hanley, Stoke-on-Trent in 1867, a generation after Hardy, in
circumstances more amenable to his ambitions. Descended from generations
of potters, Bennett senior had worked his way up from master-potter to pupil-
teacher to solicitor by age thirty-four. When the firstborn, Arnold Bennett,
arrived, the family fortunes were at a low mark; he grew up in the cramped,
unlovely quarters of a draper's and pawnbroker's shop in an industrial section
of Burslem; but by adolescence his father had qualified as a solicitor and the
family moved into a large middle-class house, their respectability secured.

Bennett was sent to the prestigious Newcastle Middle School, and although he excelled as a student, his father scotched his hopes for a university education by withdrawing him at sixteen to work in his law office. In 1888 Bennett rebelled from his servitude and went up to London. By this time journalism and literature had become regular avenues of upward mobility for men from the lower-middle class, and Bennett quickly found outlets for his talent and energy. He pursued fame and fortune avidly, unconstrained by anxieties about the "vulgarity" of ambition, and seemed to enjoy the fruits of his success with unadulterated satisfaction.[1]

The epigraphs to this chapter testify to the growing acceptance of the idea that writers were now coming from "below" and that it could be a particular strength to be unclassed, to "bridge the gulf," as Wells says.[2] Clearly the example of Hardy was important in bringing about this changing notion of the writer. Bennett feels free to address the issue of class directly in his 1909 essay "Middle Class" in which he asserts, in a tone quite foreign to Gissing or Hardy, that he was born "slightly beneath" the middle class; he expounds openly on his ambivalent relationship, concluding with the wry observation that although a writer might rail against the Philistines, he should never forget that he dines on "the bread unwillingly furnished by the enemies of art and progress."

Bennett's *Journal* and letters as well as his fiction reveal a temperament radically different from Gissing's or Hardy's. Imbued with the Protestant ethic that hard work would pay off, he had—or could pretend to—a kind of cheerful self-assurance sometimes described as cockiness. Sanguine about the prospect of democracy, he felt almost no reservations about social and political changes and little nostalgia for a more simple, ordered world of the past. He was enthusiastic about progress, excited by the technological and organizational innovations of late-Victorian capitalism, and enjoyed his liberation from the constraints of Victorian religious and moral dogma. Undisturbed by the widespread social mobility of his times, Bennett was far less concerned than Gissing or Hardy about the devaluation of culture in an increasingly democratized society; indeed, he made his reputation by appealing to the expanding middle-class reading public. Bennett was glad to be part of the modern world and perhaps a little brassy in his assurance that he was among its chief cultural arbiters. It is scarcely surprising, then, that in his fiction, ambition does not make for tragedies of exclusion, failure, or self-betrayal.

However, this public image of self-confidence and self-satisfaction, which Bennett cultivated and Ezra Pound caricatured in his portrait of Mr. Nixon, concealed a more complex, even diffident man who was from the beginning of his career conscious of two kinds of ambition. In 1894 he replied to his friend George Sturt who had offered some criticism of Bennett's first short stories.

"More continuous attention to reality" would be a fine thing. But you must remember that in order that a man sit down deliberately to be artistic, & be damned to every other consideration—he must have some inward assurance that there is a brilliant or at least pleasant conclusion to the dark tunnel which he is entering....

I may say that I have no inward assurance that I could ever do anything more than mediocre viewed strictly as art—very mediocre.

On the other hand, I have a clear idea that by cultivating that "lightness of touch" to which you refer, & exercising it upon the topicalities of the hour, I could turn out things which would be read with zest.... I would sooner succeed as a caricaturist of passing follies than fail as a producer of "documents humains." And you know if it came to an alternative between a semi-luxurious competence, & fidelity to Art, Art would have my undiminished affection—and my back.... I want my books & my pictures, & my stall at the theatre; & I want to be successful, & to mix with the fellows whose names shine in the foreheads of the magazines. Disgusting, isn't it? I think so sometimes. [3]

Sturt encouraged Bennett to work for "Art" and shrewdly noted that his "indifference... begins to look... like a false position... an artist must chuck away indifference." But if an initial lack of confidence in his own talent contributed to Bennett's willingness to compromise his artistic integrity, he could not finally resist the temptation of "a semi-luxurious competence," to be gained by exercising his talent on "the topicalities of the hour" and on the caricature of "passing follies." He believed that the material and social success which he desired required a certain prostitution of his abilities. As he matured, Bennett continued to maintain a dual conception of the artist; on the one hand he was a public apologist for the "democratisation of art," defending the virtues of best-sellers in such essays as "The 'Average Reader' and the Recipe for Popularity."[4] But he continued to hold also a fundamentally elitist concept of the artist as a detached, neutral observer of society, free from the pressures of the marketplace and honoring the obligation to present the truth through his "continuous attention to reality." In him a Reardon vied with a Milvain, and he tried to accommodate both by dividing his work into the "good" novels and the "popular" potboilers, trusting that the writer-craftsman would not be adversely affected by the writer-merchant.

Partly as a consequence of this decision to work for two masters, Art and Mammon, Bennett's fictional self-portraits fall into two types, or more precisely, into pairs of alter egos which reflect the division within the author. His first novel, *A Man from the North* (1896), is a semi-autobiographical account of a provincial youth, Richard Larch, who comes to London and attempts to be a writer only to "arrive ultimately at disillusion and a desolating suburban domesticity."[5] This same story is retold with gusto and flippancy in *The Truth about an Author,* which Bennett published anonymously in 1903, a cheerfully brash success story which debunks the mystique of being an artist.

This pair of protagonists, the one ostensibly a failure and the other a success, is repeated with variations in *The Card* and *Clayhanger;* these novels, written back to back in 1909 and 1910, are also reflections on Bennett's young manhood and recount the career of an ambitious youth in the Five Towns, Bennett's fictional version of Stoke-on-Trent. Like *The Truth about an Author, The Card* strongly suggests that success depends on a certain amount of chicanery, a mask of absolute self-confidence, and an overwhelming allegiance to Number One.[6] Without this equipment, the protagonist is doomed to decline into obscurity, to fail as an artist, to trade in his youthful dreams and hopes for an ordinary world in which human potential goes unfulfilled.

The double bind of the upwardly mobile man is evident: success requires insensitivity and a lack of integrity, but the failure to succeed in a material sense, and specifically for Bennett the failure to escape the Five Towns, is also a kind of self-betrayal. Bennett suppresses the anguish of this situation by compartmentalizing his experience. He caricatures the story of rising from the lower-middle class and escaping the provinces in *The Card* and *The Truth about an Author;* in these lighthearted, superficial versions of his success he denies both the existence of his other half, the doubtful, thoughtful self, and his anxiety about the basis for success—the trick of palming yourself off as what you are not. In *Clayhanger* and *A Man from the North,* he acknowledges that other self, but he attributes his characters' defeats to their personalities: they simply lack the superior talent, energy, and drive which Bennett knew he had. Even in his serious fiction he avoids asking whether there might be other issues at stake in a man's failure or success than individual temperament. He does not finally challenge the liberal assumption that man is free to shape his destiny as the stories of Jude Fawley and Godwin Peak, in their different ways, had done.

*   *   *

Of the novels included in this study, *Clayhanger* is the closest to the traditional Bildungsroman in moving toward an accommodation between the individual and society. However, the arena in which the protagonist attempts to realize his development is painfully restricted, for Edwin never leaves his provincial home nor is he allowed to try on a variety of work roles. The novel takes him from an adolescence fraught with conflict with his father to an intense attachment to Hilda Lessways, the dark-haired heroine who will eventually become Edwin's wife; it charts as well the family's gradual movement into the middle class. Rooted in this outwardly eventless world, Edwin dreams of escape, yearning to go to London and become an architect; instead he capitulates to his father's demand that he work in the family business. Edwin gravitates to the refined world of the upper-middle-class Orgreaves, finding in their suburban drawing rooms, and later his own, a sphere of private enrichment which compensates for the banality of the public world without. Ultimately he adjusts his dreams to reality, keeping a measure of integrity, decency, and manliness even though so many of his aspirations have been frustrated.[7]

Is it possible to see this accommodation as a resolution of the double bind? In one sense, the answer must be yes, for there is no question of the exclusion or death of the protagonist or of the corruption of his integrity. Edwin finds a *modus operandi* in the Five Towns. Indeed, in creating this character, Bennett discovers more possibilities for Edwin's inner development than he had anticipated. In *Clayhanger* he depicts a growth of the spirit and intellect that is alien to the world of *The Old Wives' Tale*. However, Bennett finally shows us an Edwin limited in his achievement: a decent, sensitive man who because of his passivity and the sheer weight of his environment abandons the strenuous and potentially alienating dream of being an artist-architect. In the story of his modest social rise, Bennett implies that a still richer life lies beyond the confines of Bursley, awaiting those who are ambitious and daring enough to climb further. At the end we are equally aware of limitations of the protagonist and limitations in his environment; and in this sense, *Clayhanger* does not so much resolve the double bind as shrink from it.

In his exploration of "the simple self that was," Bennett glimpsed the possibility of a different kind of development which would not require the protagonist to leave home, which would redefine "culture" in collective, democratic terms and redefine the artist as well. Edwin shares with the narrator some of these glimpses, but neither he nor his creator is able to develop these insights or to reconceive the dream of self-development in light of them. Both author and character turn their back on perceptions that might have led to full, integrated growth that would heal the division between the individual and society and effect a positive resolution of the double bind.

In *The Theory of the Novel* Georg Lukács describes the Bildungsroman as the highest form of prose fiction because it guides us toward a model of fruitful interaction between the individual and society, an interaction which redeems the loneliness of the dreamy idealist and the sterility of his subjective world, restoring significance to the conventional, objective world. The yearned for "reconciliation between interiority and reality" is achieved in *Wilhelm Meister,* but after Goethe, the novel of education regresses to an intermediate stage in which the protagonist achieves only a "compromise" with the world. He accepts the fact that his "desire for the essense always leads out of the world of social structures . . . and that community is possible only at the surface of life. . . ." He then accommodates himself to society by accepting its "life forms" or conventions and locks in himself the "interiority which can only be realised inside the soul."

His ultimate arrival expresses the present state of the world but is neither a protest against it nor an affirmation of it, only an understanding and experiencing of it which tries to be fair to both sides and which ascribes the soul's inability to fulfill itself in the world not only to the inessential nature of the world but also to the feebleness of the soul.

The particular weakness of this intermediate form is that the protagonist is not "exemplary":

The hero and his destiny... have no more than personal interest and the work as a whole becomes a private memoir of how a certain person succeeded in coming to terms with his world. [The events and resolutions of the novel are endowed with] the fatal, irrelevant, and petty character of the merely private.[8]

This intermediate type of the novel of education which ends in a spirit of compromise rather than positive reconciliation with the world describes *Clayhanger* admirably. Bennett once asserted that the essential quality of a novelist was "a Christ-like, all-embracing compassion"; the notion was at once his strength and limitation.[9] In *Clayhanger* he sought "to be fair to both sides," eschewing both protest and affirmation and relying instead upon a neutralizing irony which plays on the provincial world and on the "feeble soul" of Edwin. Nor can we see in the protagonist's accommodation that representative significance which could speak to the human condition. Edwin simply lacks the initiative to pursue his ambition and therefore has to accept a "compromise" with reality which is endurable because of his relatively privileged position at the end of the novel. Through his modest social rise, he enjoys enough leisure and wealth to permit a limited exercise of his "artistic sensibility"; although he is unfulfilled as an artist, the intensity of his subjective life is intended to compensate for the drabness of his social situation.

*   *   *

Part of what prevents Bennett from achieving anything more than a "compromise" was his commitment to a particular notion of the artist. It was a hegemonic notion, transmitted to Bennett by such French writers as Flaubert, the Goncourts, and Maupassant, those representatives of a Continental realist, and later naturalist, esthetic who had also influenced Gissing. For them the artist was a detached observer who withdrew from life in order to depict it disinterestedly. From this perspective the most commonplace, even sordid materials might be transformed into art. Their doctrine was attractive to a young writer who had fought to escape from provincial life only to find himself drawn back to that material in his fiction. Their emphasis on form, or "presentment" as Bennett called it, and on authorial impartiality allowed him to approach his subject matter while maintaining a critical distance. As Walter Allen observes, Bennett's setting remains "provincial" for the reader. His "attitude towards [the Five Towns] is always expository; he is explaining them, exhibiting them, to an outside world that is not provincial. They exist in relation to a larger world that Bennett accepts as the norm." For Bennett the would-be artist simply had to leave the Five Towns to achieve the appropriate distance from his subject, to see it in the proper spirit as material for art. In returning he could confer on an otherwise insignificant reality that formal significance which would redeem it. In his words, "the Usual [would be] miraculously transformed by Art into the Sublime."[10]

But this elevation of the virtue of esthetic detachment competes with another attitude in Bennett.

> Every scene, even the commonest, is wonderful, if only one can detach oneself, casting off all memory of use and custom, and behold it (as it were) for the first time; in its right, authentic colours; without making comparisons. The novelist should cherish and burnish this faculty of seeing crudely, simply, artlessly, ignorantly; of seeing like a baby or a lunatic, who lives each moment by itself and tarnishes the present by no remembrance of the past.[11]

So Bennett wrote in his *Journal* in 1897, and much of his fiction testifies to his enthusiasm for the ordinary, "commonest" scenes of life. This enthusiasm distinguishes his work from the French realists and naturalists, his early models, who approach their commonplace subject matter more in spirit of scientific detachment. From the beginning Bennett's determination to write about "the ordinary" is infused with a particular zest. In his first novel, after describing in detail a street in the London suburbs, Bennett writes:

> ...in all these things there is character and matter of interest,—truth waiting to be expounded. How many houses are there in Cartaret Street? Say eighty. Eighty theatres of love, hate, greed, tyranny, endeavour; eighty separate dramas always unfolding, intertwining, ending, beginning,—and every drama, a tragedy. No comedies, and especially no farces! Why, child, there is more character within a hundred yards of this chair than a hundred Balzacs could analyse in a hundred years.[12]

Certainly the enthusiasm is not always an asset. While he suggests the richness of experience, Bennett's inflation can rapidly become a deflation: "*every* drama, a tragedy"? There is a promiscuous quality in his relish for everything ordinary, as if Bennett literally sought to become the "baby" or "lunatic" unable to make sense out of what he sees. Moreover, such enthusiasm ultimately depends on Bennett's preserving some detachment from his subject; only the neutral observer can afford to be equally engaged by all aspects of life.

As Bennett outgrew his infatuation with realism and naturalism *à la français*, he increasingly felt that the artist needed to impose on his subject, to find some order other than a purely esthetic one, which would give significance to the depiction of reality. In 1913 in "The Author's Craft" he urged the would-be writer to observe the ordinary life around him because to do so will lead "to a better understanding of the springs of human conduct."

> Observation endows our day and our street with the romantic charm of history, and stimulates charity ... which puts itself to the trouble of understanding. The one condition is that the observer must never lose sight of the fact that what he is trying to see is life ... and not a concourse of abstractions. To appreciate all this is the first inspiring preliminary to sound observation.
>
> The second preliminary is to realise that all physical phenomena are interrelated, that there is nothing which does not bear on everything else. The whole spectacular and sensual show ... is a cause or an effect of human conduct. [13]

Bennett's criticism was far less subtle than his fictional technique, and one may readily detect in this passage the naturalist's emphasis on observation of the human world as physical phenomena. But one sees also that Bennett felt a need to do more than record experience like "a lunatic, who lives each moment by itself" and who does not connect the present with the past. In *Clayhanger,* history calls into being "the interestingness of existence" and provides a context without which the ordinary lives of the Clayhangers cannot be appreciated. [14] Bennett wants to show the interrelationships in life rather than in form—in a "concourse of abstractions." He wants to show reality as "a cause or an effect of human conduct."

That part of Bennett which responded warmly to homely materials and which sought to connect "the whole spectacular and sensual show" with human endeavor allowed him to glimpse possibilities unexplored by other writers. Despite his attachment to estheticism, he understood that art might be made out of engagement rather than withdrawal. The artist could be a mediator between alienated spheres rather than a detached observer seeking beauty through the play of his imagination. Bennett explores some of these possibilities through Edwin who, by staying in Bursley, has the chance to build connections between private and public life; between leisured and working classes; between suburb and town, city and province; between a traditional conception of culture as the domain of an elite and an emerging, democratic conception of culture as the domain of all men. Intermittently Edwin detects the possibility for a genuine reconciliation between interiority and reality, but finally he retreats from the working world to the privileged circle of the cultivated upper-middle class, which Bennett perceives as alternately stultifying and appealing. Intermittently Bennett recognizes that Edwin's limitations are related to his habit of withdrawal, to his "artistic sensibility," but the risk of conceiving of the artist as other than detached is finally too great.

It is important, then, to distinguish several quite different attitudes to "the ordinary" throughout *Clayhanger,* for they betray Bennett's uncertain attitude toward his material. There is a pervasive, usually gentle irony about Bursley and its inhabitants reflected in such touches as the place names: Duck Square or the expensive suburb of Bleakridge. This irony, as we have noted, plays on both "the inessential nature of the world" of Bursley and "the feebleness of the soul" of Edwin. There are as well the quiet remarks of a detached narrator who, by distancing himself, can see a kind of beauty in the town. There is the promiscuous enthusiasm of the neutral observer, whose insistence that things are "heroic," "grand," or "almost tragic" when we remain to be convinced, jars with the aforementioned irony. Finally there are moments when this enthusiasm is harnessed to genuine insight and Bennett is able to render convincingly the "miraculous" quality which he claims for the ordinary.[15]

Like Jude Fawley and Godwin Peak, Edwin feels himself a "born exile," a changeling misplaced at birth in surroundings that belie his inner worth, an Arnoldian "alien" aspiring to goals nobler than the shop-keeping class around him can conceive. Such inner convictions are in each case treated with considerable, but not annihilating irony. Though Edwin is spectacularly inexperienced, within him burns, as a chapter title tells us, "the flame."

> By a single urgent act of thought he would have made himself a man, and changed imperfection into perfection. He desired—and there was real passion in his desire—to do his best, to exhaust himself in doing his best, in living according to his conscience.... Achievement was not the matter of his desire: but endeavour, honest and terrific endeavour. (26)

The inhabitants of Bursley do not detect "the mysterious and holy flame of the desire for self-perfecting, blazing within that tousled head."[16] The Arnoldian language prepares us for the story of Edwin's struggle to free himself from the Hebraic, puritanical, provincial world so as to enter a Hellenic world of sweetness and light. There is no doubt about just how oppressive and stale his surroundings in many ways are. His flame is associated with his capacity to experience beauty, with his desire to be an architect, with his general curiosity about the world, and with his desire to make his own life count for something.

That he must leave school at sixteen to work in his father's print shop seems to Edwin a dreary fate for a future architect. Yet the narrator has a different perspective.

> The trickling, calm commerce of a provincial town was proceeding, bit being added to bit and item to item, until at the week's end a series of apparent nothings had swollen into the livelihood of near half a score of people. And nobody perceived how interesting it was, this interchange of activities, this ebb and flow of money, this sluggish rise and fall of reputations and fortunes, stretching out of one century into another and towards a third!... nobody heard romance in the puffing of the hidden steam engine.... (31)

Can Edwin be awakened to share Bennett's feeling for "the interestingness of existence"? Or is such interest only possible for the man no longer limited to the provincial world? Edwin's first day on the job ends with a chance opportunity to see Bursley at night in the company of his father's foreman, Big James. This tour of the town is Edwin's first adventure, his first release from the stifling petty-bourgeois respectability of his father's home, and his first experience of working-class life. At the Dragon Hotel where a Bursley cooperative society is having a purely social evening, Edwin's eyes are opened by the champion female clog-dancer.

> She danced; and the service-doorway showed a vista of open-mouthed scullions. There was no sound in the room, save the concertina and the champion clogs. Every eye was fixed on those clogs.... At intervals, with her ringed fingers she would lift the short skirt—a nothing, an imperceptibility, half an inch, with glance downcast; and the effect was profound, recondite, inexplicable. Her style was not that of a male clog-dancer, but it was indubitably clog-dancing, full of marvels to the connoisseur, and to the profane naught but a highly complicated series of wooden noises....
>
> And thus was rendered back to the people in the charming form of beauty that which the instinct of the artist had taken from the sordid ugliness of the people. The clog, the very emblem of the servitude and the squalor of brutalized populations, was changed ... into the medium of grace. Few of these men but at some time in their lives had worn the clog, had clattered in it through winter's slush ... to the manufactory and the mill and the mine.... One of the slatterns behind the doorway actually stood in clogs to watch the dancer. The clog meant everything that was harsh, foul, and desolating; it summoned images of misery and disgust. Yet on those feet ... it became the magic instrument of pleasure, waking dulled wits and forgotten aspirations, putting upon everybody an enchantment.... (88) [17]

The artist-dancer makes the oppressive, recalcitrant material world "render back" an image of "forgotten aspiration," and this union of matter and spirit ravishes all the customers as it does Edwin: "Yesterday I was at school—and today I see this!" (89). Neither irony nor unfocused enthusiasm for the spectacle of life interferes with the claim that an image of human liberation, and an experience of that liberation, is achieved with the homeliest of materials and the homeliest of audiences.

The effect of this "exquisite and vast revelation" is quickly lost on Edwin, who returns home that evening to copy some views of European capitals.

> He had chosen "View of the Cathedral of Notre-Dame, Paris, from the Pont des Arts." ... A romantic scene! He wanted to copy it exactly, to recreate it from beginning to end, to feel the thrill of producing each wonderful effect himself. Yet he sat inactive. He sat and vaguely gazed at the slope of Trafalgar Road with its double row of yellow jewels, beautifully ascending in fire to the ridge of the horizon.... and he thought how ugly and commonplace all that was, and how different from all that were the noble capitals of Europe. (91)

"How ugly and commonplace," and this not an hour after he had been "dazzled by the unforeseen chances of existence"! Of course Bennett intends us to see the irony of Edwin's blindness to the beauty of the town and to understand that he is not an artist but an imitator. But the passage betrays some blindness on Bennett's part as well. "All ugliness has an aspect of beauty. The business of the artist is to find that aspect," he had written in 1899. Granted sufficient distance one may find a certain beauty in the ordinary streetlights which appear as a "double row of yellow jewels." Bennett values this estheticizing of the commonplace and here faults Edwin for missing it. However, with the clog-dancer he had touched on something more important than the revelation of the "picturesque" in the midst of "the slovenly makeshift, shameless, filthy" town (27). The detached observer who gazes on city lights from a great height is moved to esthetic contemplation; but the vision of beauty we get through the clog-dancer arouses "aspiration" among people whom "squalor" and "servitude" have oppressed. In this scene, art is connected with freedom, and the entire scene celebrates a cultural form which is democratic rather than elitist. If we imagine the contempt that would permeate Gissing's presentation of the same scene, we can better appreciate the originality in Bennett's celebration of the ordinary.

Edwin is drawn to the Orgreaves, who represent a bourgeois ideal of cultivation based on wealth and leisure; through this family he is exposed to art, music, literature, and to an elegance and refinement that contrast sharply with the drabness of his own family's home. As a successful businessman, Darius Clayhanger eventually follows the Orgreaves to the suburb of Bleakridge and builds his first house away from the shop. This separation of work and living which signals the Clayhangers' social advance is the beginning of Edwin's determination to have a "new life" of cultivation. It is ironic (and I think unintentionally so) that the house should afford Edwin a futher insight into a democratic notion of culture. Building the house has put Edwin into "an ecstasy of contemplation." Houses had always seemed to him "superhuman [in their] awful perfection. . . . he knew that they did not build themselves. And yet, in the vagueness of his mind, he had never imaginatively realised that a house was made with hands . . . " (166).

> But now he saw. He had to see. He saw a hole in the ground . . . and the next moment that hole was a cellar. . . . He appreciated the brains necessary to put a brick on another brick, with just the right quantity of mortar in between. . . . The measurements, the rulings, the plumbings, the checkings! He was humbled and he was enlightened. He understood that a miracle is only the result of miraculous patience, miraculous nicety, miraculous honesty, miraculous perseverance. He understood that there was no golden and magic secret of building. It was just putting one brick on another and against another—but to a hair's breadth. It was just like anything else. For instance, printing! He saw even printing in a new light. (167)

The house is a "miracle," an epiphany of work, through which the ordinary, material world is connected with human creativity. "The funny thing was that the men's fingers were thick and clumsy. Never could such fingers pick up a pin! And still they would maneuver a hundredweight of timber to a pin's point" (167). As he had done with the clog-dancer, Bennett takes the very "emblem" of the worker's servile and brutalized life—his thick, clumsy fingers, ill-suited for teacups and pins—and shows how refined his work may be. "It was just like anything else." All work is potentially miraculous—potentially cultured. All around us are signs of skill and cultivation which we daily ignore, imagining that things "build themselves."

By recognizing the dimension of creativity that often goes unseen in the material world, Bennett is able to infuse ordinary men and ordinary objects and activities with significance. He shows work as a cultural activity which reconciles interiority and reality, to use Lukács's terms, and gives a new value to both the material world and the laborer. This emphasis helps to break down bourgeois conceptions about work and the working class, about a system of production that relies on division of labor, about the split between mind and body, matter and spirit.

Despite such moments when the would-be artist Edwin penetrates the mysterious objective world and the equally mysterious lower class to experience a moment of illumination, he turns away from "work" to pursue a conventional path toward self-cultivation. Obliged to abandon his dream of becoming an architect to learn his father's printing business, Edwin feels his aspirations dying and his ambition fading. He remains blind to the possibilities of developing himself through his work.

The "romance" which clings to the shop and to the "miracle" of Darius Clayhanger's career is revealed to the reader in chapter four, "The Child-Man." Drawing on a firsthand account, *When I Was a Child, By an Old Potter,* Bennett depicts the grim plight of a working-class family of the 1840s who must send the children to work at age seven and who even then do not escape the indignity, indeed the horror, of the workhouse. Standing against the side of "the Bastille," Darius's family look "like flies against a kennel." Within, Darius is separated from his parents, stripped of "his identity," dressed like dozens of pauper boys and forced to watch the spectacle of "the law" taming the instinctive revolt of a "boy-tiger."

> As the blows succeeded each other, Darius became more and more ashamed. The physical spectacle did not sicken nor horrify him, for he was a man of wide experience; but he had never before seen flogging by lawful authority. Flogging in the workshop was different, a private if sanguinary affair between free human beings. This ritualistic and cold-blooded torture was infinitely more appalling in its humiliation.... Darius knew that he was ruined ... that he was a workhouse boy for evermore. ... he would never be able to withstand the influences that had closed around him.... (45)

From this dreadful fate the family is rescued by a Sunday School teacher, Mr. Shushions, and Darius is able to begin life over in the "superb situation ... as a printer's devil." In light of his past, Darius's success in rising to own his business, a business which "the trickle of commerce" swells into a "livelihood" for himself and "half a score of others," the reader recognizes the shop as the "miracle" which Darius feels it to be. "To Darius there was no business quite like his own. He admitted that there were businesses much bigger, but they lacked the miraculous quality that his own had. They were not sacred. His was, genuinely" (142).

The shop is a monument to human freedom, built not out of greed or a lack of imagination but out of Darius's will to safeguard his human dignity. Like the clog-dancer and the house, it is a fusion of aspiration and material reality, but unlike them, it has a history in this novel: the symbol of Darius's freedom becomes his son's prison. Because of his father's pride, Edwin never knows the history which would illuminate the shop and his father's life for him.

> Darius had never spoken to a soul of his night in the Bastille. All his infancy was his own fearful secret. His life, seen whole, had been a miracle. But none knew that except himself and Mr Shushions. Assuredly Edwin never even faintly suspected it. To Edwin Mr Shushions was nothing but a feeble and tedious old man. (46)

Darius's career reveals some of the contradictions of capitalist society. The "child-man," whose fierce independence and determination to insist on his own dignity provide the energy for his upward mobility, deteriorates in his later years into a petty tyrant who has no respect for his children's rights or freedom. The struggle for success has made him a tightfisted, unyielding businessman, hardly able to enjoy the fruits of his wealth and miserly to his family. His authority over his children ends with the degrading senility of his long illness. On his deathbed, "with his pimpled face and glaring eyes, his gleaming gold teeth, his frowziness of a difficult invalid, his grimaces and gestures which were the results of a lifetime devoted to gain, he made a loathsome object" (379). His resolve to insure his own dignity takes shape, in the bourgeois world, as the single-minded pursuit of money. His dedication to freedom is reified into a pursuit of the wealth which becomes the foundation for the relative luxury in which his children live, lacking any appreciation of its origin in spirit. Out of the worker emerges the petty bourgeois, and out of him the refined, in some ways effete "aristocrat" Edwin, who eventually joins the upper-middle class. The ideals of the bourgeois revolution and the dissolution of those ideals are exposed in the career of Darius, which forms the background for his son's education. In the estrangement of father and son, we see in microcosm the estrangement of the working and leisured classes—and society's ignorance of the processes by which wealth and then cultivation are generated.

Although he has fictionally realized some of the historical contradictions which have shaped Darius's career, Bennett does not pursue their development in Edwin. In particular he ignores the contradiction that the bourgeois revolution (which began with the premise that every man had a subjective ideal of freedom, an interiority, which he ought to be free to realize in reality) has created a privileged class which arrogates a disproportionate part of the material base of freedom. This class justifies its dominance in part by denying that the working class possesses that interiority, that subjective world of value, which gives dignity and meaning to a man's life and work. Culture, deriving from the exercise of subjectivity, becomes a value which legitimates the hegemony of the middle classes, whose version of culture is dependent upon wealth, leisure, and an inherited standard of taste.

Bennett's narrator appears to accept the qualitative distinction which Edwin perceives between himself and his father: "an ugly, undistinguished, and somewhat vulgar man" (93). For his part, Darius thinks:

> ... there was something about Edwin that [he] admired, even respected and envied ... a personal distinction that he himself could never compass. Edwin talked more correctly than his father. He thought differently from his father. He had an original grace. *In the essence of his being he was superior to both his father and his sisters.* ... Darius was ... puzzled how he, so common, had begotten a creature so subtly aristocratic. ... (94, emphasis added)

In this passage Darius's perceptions seem to melt into the narrator's just at the point of a disturbing shift where superficial difference ("talked more correctly") becomes a qualitative distinction ("in the essence of his being he was superior"). Later the narrator asserts that the new house is "in emotional fact [Edwin's] because he alone was capable of possessing it by enjoying it. ... To the plebeian in Darius it was of course grandiose, and vast; to Edwin also, in a lesser degree. But to Edwin it was not a house, it was a work of art, it was an emanation of the soul" (164).

Bennett recognizes that Edwin's refinement depends on his father's labor and draws our attention to the son's blindness.

> It was nothing to Edwin that Darius owned [the house] and nearly everything in it. He was generally nervous in his father's presence, and his submissiveness only hid *a spiritual independence* that was not less fierce for being restrained. He thought Darius a gross, fleshly organism, *as he indeed was,* and he privately objected to many paternal mannerisms, of eating, drinking, breathing, eructation, speech, deportment, and garb. (246, emphasis added)

Edwin's refinement is ironic in the context of his blithe dismissal of the economic base of his cultivated delicacy. Yet the narrator appears to share (in the italicized phrases) the son's relegation of Darius from human to "organism"; in claiming a "spiritual independence" for Edwin, the narrator again suggests a qualitative distinction between father and son.

Of Osmond Orgreave, who becomes something of a mentor in Edwin's quest for self-development, the narrator says "his social and moral superiority [to Darius], his real aloofness, remained absolutely unimpaired. The clear image of him as a fine gentleman was never dulled nor distorted ... " (163). The facile phrase, "social and moral superiority" in which the adjectives seem mutually to justify each other is disappointing in a novel which elsewhere questions the basis for such judgments. It is not clear why we should believe that the agreeable Osmond is morally superior to Darius. He is a diligent provider for an extravagant family, a hard-driving businessman who can get the better of Darius at times, a genial parent. Edwin admires him for his "aristocratic deportment" and his ability to keep "his dignity and his distance during encounters with Darius" (166), but this hardly constitutes the grounds for moral superiority. While the narrator is mildly ironic in describing Orgreave's business methods, nothing seriously undermines the aura of the "gentleman." As an architect, Orgreave is obliged to "hawk" land and then persuade

> the purchaser that if he wished to retain the respect of the community he must put on the plot a house worthy of the plot. The Orgreave family all had expensive tastes, and it was Osmond Orgreave's task to find most of the money needed for the satisfaction of those tastes. He always did find it, because the necessity was upon him, but he did not always find it easily.... Undoubtedly the clothes on Janet's [his daughter's] back were partly responsible for the celerity with which building land at Bleakridge was "developed."...(162)

Surely Darius's creation of an independent business is more of an "emanation of the soul" than these new suburban houses, built to satisfy the urge for social status? The narrator who gives us that earlier perspective on Darius and who sees the element of conspicuous consumption in the Orgreaves' lifestyle nevertheless continues to claim an inner superiority for those whose principal advantage is that they are at least one generation removed from the workhouse. Moreover, at times Bennett seems to be captivated with what money can buy. The Orgreaves' home offers Edwin a "vision...of the possibilities of being really interested in life. He saw new avenues towards joy" (202). "The general effect [of the Orgreaves' drawing room] was of extraordinary lavish profusion—of wilful, splendid, careless extravagance" (190). Not only Edwin is impressed; the narrator continues:

> ...the room was *historic;* it had been the *theatre of history.* For twenty-five years...it had witnessed the *adventurous* domestic career of the Orgreaves, so quiet superficially, so *exciting* in reality. It was the drawing-room of a man who had consistently used immense powers of industry for the satisfaction of his prodigal instincts.... Spend and gain! And, for a change, gain and spend! That was the method.... Satisfy your curiosity and your other instincts! Experiment! Accept risks!... Play with the same intentness as you work! Live to the uttermost instant and to the last flicker of energy! Such was the spirit of Osmond Orgreave....(190, emphasis added)

In the italicized words we hear that unsubstantiated enthusiasm of the neutral observer, too ready to see drama and history in any random event. As the passage continues, we realize that Bennett is genuinely excited by the use of "immense powers of industry for the satisfaction of . . . prodigal instincts." "Spend and gain!" That's how one lives "to the uttermost." It is disappointing that such a life should so attract a man capable of profound insight into the real drama of history and into activities which redeem our lives from mere "getting and spending." Orgreave's conspicuous consumption is but the reverse of Darius's miserliness, not an alternative way of life which gives meaning to the material world by infusing it with value. And Edwin, essentially unchanged by his insights into the working community of Bursley, centers his "new life" at Bleakridge in the book-lined study in which he hoards, as much as Darius ever did, his own treasure.

Bennett is torn. He can see in common lives and common objects a union of human aspiration and matter, of interiority and reality, which gives value and integrity to human experience. He can see that aspiration is a democratic quality, that work is potentially a cultivated activity, and that ordinary men and women struggle to realize beauty and freedom in their lives and works. Such insights suffuse his understanding of the clog-dancer, the building of the house, and the development of Darius's career. At the same time he wants to maintain the legitimacy of an upper-middle-class elite by affirming that men of this class possess a superior sensibility, a "spiritual independence," in contrast to the brutalized plebeians, and he implies that such inner superiority is an essential quality of being, not created by material conditions.

Were Edwin's development to be "exemplary" in Lukács's sense, he would have had to face some sharp contradictions, in particular the growing estrangement between the wealthy leisured class, to which Edwin belongs at the end of the novel, and the working class from which he has indirectly sprung. He would either suffer from or have tried to heal the alienation between suburb and town, culture and work, individual subjectivity and social reality. Such a career might have discovered a new avenue for self-development, a new conception of Bildung. Instead, Bennett retires Edwin to the sidelines with those who view struggle and social change from afar. He rescues Edwin from the course of history, justifies his move into a privileged elite on the grounds of his "artistic sensibility," and tries to convince us that an intense subjective life can compensate for a banal existence.

Bennett implicitly argues that the artist has a unique, privileged way of coming to terms with reality. For him the artist escapes the flux of time to a vantage point from which he surveys history and is no longer its subject. Thus all events are "interesting" to him, though he is engaged by none. He does not try to make his active experience in the world meaningful; instead he retreats to a subjective experience of freedom and a symbolic reconciliation of interiority and reality achieved in art or in moments of esthetic contemplation. The social extension of this argument—that art and the artist redeem an otherwise banal reality—is that the leisured class, represented by the Orgreaves and Edwin, is justified in occupying its privileged position because of its fine sensibility. Bennett supports this claim even though he has shown the historical and material processes which bring that sensibility into being, even though he has shown that the urge to reconcile matter and spirit exists in working people whose labor is exploited to create luxury.

*   *   *

The chapters on the Sunday School Centenary have been widely admired. Here the close observation of provincial life amounts to much more than a Derby Day canvas. The crowd scene allows scope for Bennett's presentation of the social, religious, and economic life of the town as the background which has formed his characters in ways they do not know. These chapters also provide an occasion to examine Edwin's habit of remaining aloof. The narrator has earlier referred to "the impartial and unmoved spectator that sat somewhere in Edwin, as in everybody who possesses artistic sensibility, watching his secret life as from a conning tower" (219). Here he explores the roots of Edwin's detachment, his fear of experience and of the press of human flesh. The chapters constitute an insightful psychological study of this artist manqué, a study that perhaps owed something to self-examination. In them Bennett presents Edwin's commitment to a self-aware independence and rationality alongside his fear of submersion in the mass and in the irrational. It is a thoughtful examination of a young man's reaction to his community.

A minor character, Mr. Shushions, has already provided an occasion for contrasting the childhoods of father and son and thus exploring the gulf between them. He is introduced in the first pages of the novel where Edwin is merely puzzled by his father's unusual deference to the old man; the reader there learns about the critical role which this Sunday School teacher had played in saving Darius. We also learn how much Sunday School had meant to the boy of seven for whom it was the only respite from the dirt and monotony of work, the sole opportunity to become literate. Mr. Shushions does not return until the chapters on the Sunday School Centenary, at which occasion he is to be honored as "the oldest Sunday School teacher." Here he serves to dramatize how history is forgotten by the townsfolk, even during the centenary, and how it is ignored by both Darius and Edwin.

The son has no inkling of the role which Sunday Schools and Shushions have played in his family's history; he knows only that his own experience of religious education is associated "with atrocious tedium, pietistic insincerity, and humiliating contacts" (213). With the Orgreaves he disparages the celebration, finding the preparation for the ceremonies tawdry and embarrassing. But despite himself, "the gathering force of public opinion had been changing his attitude.... the derision was mysteriously transformed into an inimical respect. By what? By he knew not what. By something without a name in the air which the mind breathes" (213). For all his wish to set himself apart from the pietistic gathering and from his family who are caught up in the festivities, Edwin is moved in spite of himself. He cannot escape the "air" which his mind breathes even though he struggles to maintain his separateness.

Walking into the square with Hilda Lessways, whom he has met at the Orgreaves, he feels as if the crowd has "no more in common with himself and her than animals had." Feeling as if he "had been lifted up to splendid ease above the squalid and pitiful human welter" (225), he rents barrels so that he and Hilda may see over the heads of the crowd into the square where a huge banner lettered "The Blood of the Lamb" waves in the breeze while a brass band plays "Rock of Ages." "The volume of sound was overwhelming. Its crashing force was enough to sweep people from barrels. Edwin could feel moisture in his eyes, and he dared not look at Hilda. 'Why the deuce do I want to cry?' he asked himself angrily, and was ashamed" (229). The combination of the beautiful, popular hymns with their emotionally charged imagery of bathing in the blood of the Lamb and the communal celebration of faith is almost enough to sweep Edwin off his barrel, to bring him down into the crowd and indeed down to his roots. But he is sorely troubled by the conflicting emotions he feels. As a rationalist and agnostic (for so he has announced himself to Hilda only the previous evening), the declaration of a collective, mystical faith repels him. "He saw the meek, stupid, and superstitious faces, all turned one way, all for the moment under the empire of one horrible idea, all convinced that the consequences of sins could be prevented by an act of belief, all gloating over inexhaustible tides of blood." But he is also beginning to feel in himself the sexual stirring he associates with the crowd; he wants to "trample on [Hilda's] feelings [because] she roused the brute in him, and perhaps no one was more astonished than himself to witness the brute stirring" (231). To keep near that "unmoved spectator" in himself, he mocks the lyrics, ("More blood!" he whispers to Hilda) only to be surprised by her passionate defense: "That's the most splendid religious verse ever written!" Challenging him to name the author, she sneers at his ignorance of Dr. Watts.

In Edwin the desire for individuality strains against his "social instinct" and his bond with the community. Intellectual convictions combine with sexual anxiety (evoked by the passionate eroticism of the hymns) and the wish to set himself socially apart from the crowd. He is embarrassed by his own nature, the "brute" in him which he would tame with the reason, reserve, and intellect which mark him as a superior man. But for all his aloofness he is still moved by hymns which he knows by heart and which are, of course, the work of a great and popular poet. Hilda surprises him by drawing his attention to the distinguished tradition to which Dr. Watts belongs and by her admiration for the belief which informs the art. Like Edwin, she is cut off from conventional religion but is looking for new connections between passion and intelligence.

From their vantage point on their barrels, Edwin and Hilda see old Mr. Shushions struggling toward the platform, being mocked by some youngsters. To Edwin, who does not recognize him, Shushions appears to be "Time's obscene victim," a horrifying image of what he too will become; for his own sake as much as for Shushions, Edwin wants to restore a measure of his dignity. But it is Hilda who jumps down into the crowd, protecting the old man and persuading him gently to the platform. The tableau of her leaning over the old man, her hand on his shoulder, "was a vision [that] remained one of the epochal things of [Edwin's] existence" (237).

This last phrase provides an instance of the difficulty in determining Bennett's tone. Is Edwin's "vision" genuinely "epochal"—a moment when chance and the artist's eye combine to infuse the commonplace with beauty? Or is there ironic inflation, implying that Edwin's life is so thin that such a moment looms as "epochal"? One would guess the former, and yet the tone of the final paragraph suggests that Edwin's response is radically inadequate.

> Thus was the doddering old fool [Shushions] who had given his youth to Sunday schools when Sunday schools were not patronized by princes, archbishops, and lord mayors, when Sunday schools were the scorn of the intelligent, and had sometimes to be held in public-houses for lack of better accommodation—thus was he taken off for a show and a museum curiosity by indulgent and shallow Samaritans who had not even the wit to guess that he had sown what they were reaping. And Darius Clayhanger stood oblivious at a high window of the sacred Bank. And Edwin, who, all unconscious, owed the very fact of his existence to the doting imbecile, regarded him chiefly as a figure in a tableau, as the chance instrument of a woman's beautiful revelation. Mr Shushions' sole crime against society was that he had forgotten to die. (238)

With scornful irony the narrator charges the townspeople at large and Darius and Edwin in particular with failing to see that they reap what others have sown. In remaining aloof and "oblivious," both father and son fail in a moral obligation to the old man, "the doddering old fool." (Is this phrase an ironic vocalization of Edwin's view or the narrator's own view?) Darius, who does know what he owes, will pay heavily. His breakdown and fatal decline are triggered shortly after the Centenary when he learns that Shushions has died, neglected, in the workhouse. Edwin is never to understand why the old man's death has affected his father so seriously nor to feel that Shushions is anything more to him than "the chance instrument" of an intimate revelation. But in paralleling the "obliviousness" of father and son, the narrator surely implies that Edwin has missed a revelation of wider significance—the revelation of his own connection with the past and with other people. Standing above the crowd, Edwin turns history into tableaux, into moments that purport to make ordinary life "epochal," memorialized, estheticized, redeemed. He substitutes contemplation for action. Shushions' ordinary life involved an act which returned freedom to Darius. That he should end by becoming grist for Edwin's subjective experience suggests that something has gone mightily wrong. And yet rather than keep the focus on Edwin's inadequacy, the narrator shifts in the last sentence to quite a different ironic perspective which had informed *The Old Wives' Tale*. The distinction between action and contemplation is replaced with the almost indifferent realization that all men must eventually die, that the only real "crime" is in failing to give in to that inevitability. Mr. Shushions is worth more than that last, throwaway line. Although the narrator treats Edwin's diffidence with critical irony in these chapters, his retreat to a subjective world of intense private experience ultimately will be accepted as a substitute for engagement with reality.

The one person who might be able to lead Edwin down into the crowd is Hilda. She provides a delightful example of the way in which experience invades and enhances our narrow, subjective world. She fascinates Edwin because she corresponds to no image in his mind; she represents the lure of reality and its promise of an enrichment beyond what he can imagine. Her presence at his side makes him conscious of the conflicts between his own repressed passion, which he associates with the lower classes, and the cultivation of mind and sensibility, which he associates with the Orgreaves. In Hilda he recognizes a connection between the two realms: "She could be passionate concerning Victor Hugo," he recalls, while vividly remembering how her "spirit" works on his body: she "rouse[s] the brute in him," and in this way she invites him into the world of experience, invites him to unify his own passion and intellect. Under her influence, Edwin becomes aware of the aridity of his private existence: "She was alive in every particle of herself. She gave off antipathies as a liquid gives off vapour" (225). Hilda stimulates in him a sense of heightened contradictions demanding resolution.

Unfortunately as he develops their relationship, Bennett increasingly ignores the connections between the social and personal worlds. He romanticizes Hilda as the "Unknown," allowing her to become a substitute for experience instead of a way into reality. The social and political worlds become scene-painting against which their love affair is played out. When they next meet, fifteen months later, a strike is on, and Edwin tells Hilda, "workmen on strike are always in the right; at bottom I mean. You've only got to look at them in a crowd together. They don't starve themselves for fun" (264). When they go to the Blood Tub where the workers are meeting, characteristically it is Hilda who insists that they go in, but they both enter as spectators who see not men but animals.

Hands clawed at the interrupter and dragged him with extreme violence to the level of the bench, where he muttered like a dying volcano. Angry howls shot up here and there, snappish, menacing, and bestial.... There was more interruption. The dangerous growls continued in running explosions along the benches. (283)

The meeting ends with the singing of "Rock of Ages," and Edwin and Hilda "escape" "as before a flood.... The crowd came surging out of the narrow neck of the building and spread over the pavements like a sinister liquid" (283–84). The images connect this scene with all that was unsettling to Edwin in the Centenary, but here we are completely sympathetic with his retreat. Once they are safe in the shop, Hilda's compassion for the men becomes part of her attraction for Edwin, as his is for her. While liberal sympathies may be admirable, these protagonists are never required to act on them; they are never required to confront their ideals with reality. Indeed, their private relationship becomes a substitute for such a confrontation.

The full extent of this privatization of experience is revealed in *These Twain,* part three of *The Clayhanger Trilogy.* Here Hilda and Edwin continue their retreat from the working community, moving from the suburbs to a country house. Edwin accepts as inevitable the gulf between his ideals and reality.

Now the whole mass seemed to be rising, under the action of some strange leaven, and those few who by intelligence, by manners, or by money counted themselves select were fleeing as from an inundation. Edwin had not meant to join in the exodus. But he too would join it. Destiny had seized him. Let him be as democratic in spirit as he would, his fate was to be cut off from the democracy, with which, for the rest, he had very little of speech or thought or emotion in common, but in which, from an implacable sense of justice, he was religiously and unchangeably determined to put his trust.[18]

John Lucas's criticism of *These Twain* is admirable: "There is about the novel a dominant or determined complacency that severely damages its worth." Hilda attempts to suppress the dissatisfactions of her role as a married woman of leisure by buying a bigger house and by organizing "social distractions" for the overworked Edwin. He in turn works, as Orgreave had, for the gratification he feels in satisfying his wife's expensive tastes:

... fundamentally, she was the cause of the business; it was all for her; it existed with its dirt, noise, crudity, strain and eternal effort so that she might exist in her elegance, her disturbing femininity, her restricted and deep affections, her irrational capriciousness, and her strange, brusque commonsense.

Edwin satisfies his social conscience by voting the liberal ticket, thinking "pretty well of himself as a lover of his fellow men," but his relish for "the adventure of existence" derives solely from his relationship to Hilda. Social, moral, and political questions are never put to any test. As Lucas notes: "The result is that the essential sterility of Edwin's life passes unnoticed. Or unremarked. For I can't believe that Bennett didn't know, deep down, how sterile it was. . . . But something equally deep within him prevented him blowing the gaff on it."[19]

This "essential sterility" is already evident in *Clayhanger* where we can see Bennett's willingness to confine "the adventure of existence" to the private, subjective world in order to avoid any disturbing confrontation with the social order. What Bennett calls the "core" experiences of love and death are played out against the background of the upward mobility of the family, of strikes, elections, the Home Rule debate and the breakup of the Liberal Party, but "the whole spectacular and sensual show" is not a unified vision in which the physical and social phenomena are interrelated, in which private experience is connected to social reality. Edwin's dinner with the Felons, a group of solidly Tory Rotarians, immediately precedes his long night vigil over his dying father, as though to make the point that the private, "core" experiences are necessarily more central and more humanizing than politics.

Edwin's life declines to the ordinary, in the sense of the private and inessential, the banal and commonplace. His pursuit of culture among the upper-middle class is a withdrawal which the novel shows to be stultifying. Shut up in his study after business hours, Edwin works toward "his great end of self-perfecting" (175) by a course of reading, dimly aware that life has lost its "zest." At one point in particular Bennett acknowledges how vacuous is this ideal of cultivation which offers a narcotic to dull the ache of an insignificant existence.

> Despite his genuine aspirations, despite his taste which was growing more and more fastidious, [Edwin] found it exceedingly difficult to proceed with his regular plan of reading while there was an illustrated magazine unexplored. Besides, the name of *Harper's* was august. To read *Harper's* was to acquire merit; even the pictures in *Harper's* were too subtle for the uncultivated. . . . Unlike the magazines of his youth, its aim was to soothe and flatter, not to disconcert and impeach. He looked at the refined illustrations of South American capitals and of picturesque corners in Provence . . . and he tried to slip into the rectified and softened world offered by the magazine. . . . He wanted the illusions of *Harper's*. He desired the comfort, the distraction, and the pleasant ideal longings which they aroused. (334, 337–38)

At thirty Edwin is no more self-aware than when he copied views of European capitals at sixteen. In moving to Bleakridge and otherwise cutting himself off from Bursley, Edwin has shut his eyes to the "miracle" of living culture which can transform the ordinary world. All the *Harper's* magazines and volumes of philosophy, and even the intensity of "core" experiences, cannot stave off the emptiness of this inward turning from work and community. Bennett almost "blows the gaff," but finally he wants to pretend that in this combination of upper-middle-class culture and an intense, subjective life nothing essential has been lost. By stressing the cultivation of subjectivity as the most valuable human activity, Bennett justifies the choices he made in his own life and justifies, too, the continued existence of a leisured elite. He refuses to see that the missed opportunity lies not in Edwin's failure to become an artist but in his failure to mediate between private and public life, between middle and working classes, between the old ideal of culture, based on leisure, money, and an inherited standard of taste, and the new ideal of culture as any significant transformation of the material world through a vision of human freedom.

Committed to a particular conception of the artist as an impartial spectator rather than a participant in life, Bennett could not envision any alternative other than compromise for Edwin. For author and character, the artist finally remains a superior being who escapes from history into the perfection of esthetic form, that escape being justified by his superior sensibility. Such a conception justified the course of Bennett's own life, his departure from Burslem and his own withdrawal into the privileged world of metropolitan, upper-middle-class culture. We can see his portrait of a sensitive young man as an explanation and a justification for Bennett's choice to leave the provincial working world; but it also registers doubts about that choice and intuitions about a potentially different resolution. Although Bennett maintained that only the artist who escaped from the provinces could achieve more than a compromise with life, a good deal in *Clayhanger* suggests that a novel of education should end not in the metropolis but in the Five Towns, where a genuine reconciliation of interiority and reality might be achieved; its hero would not be a traditionally aloof artist but a mediator immersed in life and sensitive to the historical contradictions of his time.

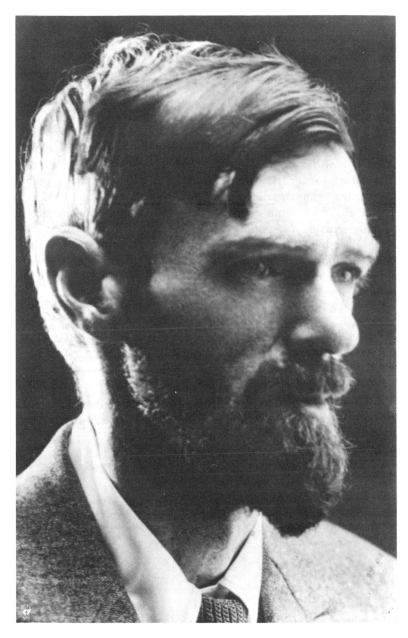

Figure 4.   D. H. Lawrence, 1929
*(Photograph by P. Juley & Son; Reprinted courtesy of the National
Portrait Gallery, London)*

4

Lawrence: Climbing Up

When you climb up to the middle classes
you leave a lot behind you,
you leave a lot, you've lost a lot
and you've nobody to remind you
of all the things they squeezed out of you
when they took you and refined you.
                    "Climbing Up" from *Pansies* (1929)

While Bennett might speak in polite tones of his deep-seated hostility to the middle class, Lawrence puts into plain English his resentment about his upward mobility. This is but one of half a dozen "pansies" which indicate how searing the experience must have been. "Finding Your Level," "A Rise in the World," "The Saddest Day," "Up He Goes!"—the titles register the bitter sarcasm this subject prompts from Lawrence.[1] Written in 1928 near the end of his life, these poems, like the three versions of *Lady Chatterley's Lover,* suggest that Lawrence never worked through the conflict he felt in himself between bourgeois and laborer.

Two autobiographical sketches, also written in the late 1920s, confirm this impression. In both Lawrence insists on his working-class background. His father was "a collier, and only a collier, nothing praiseworthy about him. He wasn't even respectable. . . . " He was "scarcely able to read or write—Mother [was] from the bourgeoisie, the cultural element in the house." "She spoke King's English, without an accent," read and wrote well, "[b]ut she was a working man's wife, and nothing else. . . . " At twelve Lawrence won a scholarship to the "purely bourgeois" Nottingham High School and was "quite happy there, but the scholarship boys were a class apart—D.H. . . . instinctively recoiled away from the bourgeoisie. . . . [He] recoiled away from the world, hated its ladder, & refused to rise." Intending to be a schoolteacher, he wrote poems and stories "without any idea of becoming a literary man at all." His

success "all happened by itself and without any groans from me.... The girl
had launched me, so easily, on my literary career, like a princess cutting a
thread, launching a ship," he reminisces, referring to Jessie Chambers's role in
submitting some of his work to Ford Madox Hueffer. The upshot of this
success is that Lawrence now feels estranged.

> Whether I get on *in* the world is a question; but I certainly don't get on very well *with* the
> world.... I don't feel there is any very cordial or fundamental contact between me and
> society, or me and other people. There is a breach [which has] something to do with class.
> Class makes a gulf, across which all the best human flow is lost. It is not exactly the triumph
> of the middle classes that has made the deadness, but the triumph of the middle-class *thing*.
>   As a man from the working class, I feel that the middle class cut off some of my vital
> vibration when I am with them....
>   I cannot make the transfer from my own class into the middle class. I cannot... forfeit my
> passional consciousness and my old blood-affinity... for that other thin, spurious mental
> conceit which is all that is left of the mental consciousness once it has made itself exclusive.

The sketches reveal important, often contradictory attitudes to his
experience of upward mobility. In both Lawrence suggests that not only did he
come from the working class, he still belongs to it in spirit. He has "refused to
rise." And on the other hand "it all happened by itself." In what we will see as a
characteristic metaphor, he imagines himself as an inert "ship" launched by a
"princess." As Hardy had done in his autobiography, Lawrence insists that his
success has come effortlessly, without an act of will. His social rise has cut him
off from a sense of community and connectedness which he now associates
with his working-class home. The "old blood-affinity" of one class is clearly
opposed to the mental consciousness appropriated (and turned into mere
"conceit") by the middle class. Despite the note of bravado in claiming to be
working-class, Lawrence recognizes that he can't go home again. "Why don't I
live with my working people? Because their vibration is limited in another
direction. They are narrow... in outlook, in prejudice, and narrow in
intelligence. This again makes a prison. One can belong absolutely to no
class."[2]
    One can readily see that Lawrence's major themes grow out of his
experience in being unclassed. The desire for individuation is associated with
his petty-bourgeois mother whose class background made her, as he notes in
the sketches, "superior" and "different"; the desire for connection is associated
with his early sense of community in a working-class family, a community lost
to Lawrence when he began his climb into the bourgeoisie. In his fiction he
sought to reconcile the values associated with both parents—the pride in
individual achievement and the participation in a community. The symbol of
that reconciliation is often marriage or a sexual relationship within which each
partner gains a vivid sense of "inter-relatedness" while maintaining an equally

vivid sense of his individuality. In his fiction, sex is often the meeting ground for two classes: *The White Peacock, Sons and Lovers, The Rainbow, The Lost Girl, Aaron's Rod,* and *Lady Chatterley's Lover* are cases in point among the novels; "Odour of Chrysanthemums," "Daughters of the Vicar," "The Princess," "The Prussian Officer," and "You Touched Me," among the short stories. Through sex Lawrence attempts to unite working class and bourgeoisie, to heal the division between body and mind, to balance blood consciousness and mental consciousness, and to accommodate the need for individuality and the need for community.

Often Lawrence seems to turn his back on society, finding in sex a subjective freedom, a psychic balance unrelated to and independent of the social and material world—a private resolution of conflicting ideologies. In Lawrence's Bildungsromane, sexual experience preempts traditional avenues to self-realization. Two of his finest novels, *Sons and Lovers* (1913) and *The Rainbow* (1915), are semi-autobiographical, but in neither does Lawrence dramatize his own movement out of the working class and the restricted, provincial world of the Midlands. By making sexual experience the avenue to true selfhood, he ignores the trauma of upward mobility; sex affords his characters a way of attaining a full experience of individuality without costly estrangement, guilt, self-betrayal, or disillusionment.

Lawrence's sexual Bildung allowed him to ignore the importance of social institutions and formations in stimulating the desire for a heightened sense of identity and in providing the means of achieving it. Moreover, his sexual Bildung provided the basis for a new, classless elite of the initiate, of which Lawrence was the founding member, and led him to mystify the concepts of individuation and connection so that both have a presocial character. However, even when his characters seem most removed from social reality, their sexual relationships recapitulate the fundamental conflict between bourgeois individualism and working-class communalism. In Lawrence, the social double bind of the upwardly mobile man is translated into the psycho-sexual problem of achieving identity within a sexual relationship that guarantees connection. From this perspective we see that like Gissing, Hardy, and Bennett, Lawrence could not imagine a satisfying closure for the homeless, unclassed man.[3]

*   *   *

Lawrence cheats about the story of his adolescence; the spirit of rebellion brought with it a shame not only of his shames but of his happiness. The suppressed secret is that the pressure of Paul's environment made him a snob. He half admits it, but only in discussion. It is never enacted. Imagine Stendhal, the supreme portrayer of very young men in European literature, missing that![4]

V. S. Pritchett's comment on *Sons and Lovers* reminds us that although in many respects this novel of adolescent development is frank and revealing, Lawrence almost entirely omits the story of his education, his pupil-teaching and scholarship to Nottingham University College, his move to London, and his gradual separation from the community of his birth.[5] Very little of the pride and ambition, the sense of release, and the sheer "happiness" which the young Lawrence must have felt as he made his way up the educational ladder and found his footing as a promising young writer find their way into the novel. In *Sons and Lovers* Lawrence ignored the break that he had already made with his past to explore sexual experience as an avenue to individuation. He makes Paul an exceptionally passive protagonist who has virtually to be pushed out of the nest.

Here as elsewhere in his early fiction Lawrence's women, rather than men, are ambitious. From the moment of birth onward women push men into the world. In urging them toward individuation and separation, women stimulate an unhealthy mental consciousness; they demand that men control their sexual desires in order to put their energies into social advance. Such an argument relieves Lawrence of some of the responsibility for his separation from Eastwood and the break he made with family and sweethearts. Sex is a way of rebelling against the demands of women and a way of avoiding—indeed of counteracting—the mechanization and materialism of industrial civilization. But sex is also a way of realizing values which Lawrence shares with women, specifically the value of expanding one's powers and becoming what he calls elsewhere "the poppy self."[6]

In his female characters—Gertrude Morel, Miriam, and Clara—Lawrence admirably represents how individuality, aspiration, ambition, and petty-bourgeois consciousness are bound together. While Paul is drawn to these women, he is not supposed to share their restless dissatisfaction with the narrow, provincial world. Gertrude Morel's desire to dissociate herself from her neighbors is woven into the very texture of Lawrence's presentation of the working-class community. Few badges of status are available to her, but she maintains a little strip of garden which sets her apart from her neighbors, has chats with the vicar, and reads papers on social issues before the Women's Guild. "It seemed queer to the children to see their mother, who was always busy about the house, sitting, writing...thinking, referring to books, and writing again. They felt for her on such occasions the deepest respect."[7] Both of her elder sons share the mother's sense of distinction, her tastes and standards, and her aspiration for an informed and self-reflective life beyond the range of most of the inhabitants of Bestwood. Both enter the world of trade as her "knights," the word invoking a romantic aura around the mundane activity of rising socially. But the dangers which attend ambition are registered in William's career—in his exhausting struggle, his separation from home, and his lonely death in a London flat.

Like Paul's mother, Miriam wants to rise above the restrictive world to which class and sex have consigned her. Education is her avenue of self-development and also a way of maintaining social distance: an escape and a barrier. She is

> a princess turned into a swine-girl in her own imagination.... She could not be a princess by wealth or standing. So she was made to have learning whereon to pride herself. For she was different from other folk, and must not be scooped up among the common fry. Learning was the only distinction to which she thought to aspire.... She must have something to reinforce her pride, because she felt different from other people. (143)

Through education, those excluded by money and class may achieve a measure of personal distinction which will command "respect"; they can establish a division between the self, which already feels "different," and "the vulgarity of the other choir-girls and ... the common-sounding voice of the curate" (142). In *The Rainbow,* Ursula is another swine-girl princess, and the similarity in the depiction of these two girls (especially given how closely Ursula's career parallels Lawrence's) suggests that the author is projecting some of his own feelings of superiority and entrapment in his female characters.[8]

Paul shares with his mother and sweetheart their conviction of innate superiority, which occasionally does manifest itself as snobbery, as in the scene in which he picks up his father's weekly earnings and is twitted by the paymaster. To his mother he bursts out, "They're hateful, and common, and hateful.... Mr. Braithwaite drops his 'h's,' and Mr. Winterbottom says 'You was'" (72). From his mother Paul has learned to distinguish himself from his environment and to do so in innumerable ways which betray his awareness of class differences. But Lawrence more often treats Paul's sense of superiority as something apart from ordinary class-consciousness, unrelated to ambition or to any need to be recognized in the world's eye. Paul is ostensibly not interested in rising out of the working class. When he leaves school at fourteen, his mother asks, "What do you want to be?" and he responds, "Anything," which, as she shrewdly notes, is "no answer" (88). He takes refuge in a passive nondefinition of self which seems like indifference to his social status but which hides his privately held belief in his difference and his reluctance to test his ambition in a competitive world. He is torn between the desire to be "someone" and his dread of leaving home. The prospect of a job is like "being taken into bondage. His freedom in the beloved home valley was going now" (89). Copying newspaper advertisements in the library, he sees a passing waggoner almost asleep on his cart. "Paul wished he were stupid. 'I wish ... I was fat like him, and like a dog in the sun. I wish I was a pig and a brewer's waggoner'" (90). His diffidence is reminiscent of the young Hardy who wanted to retreat under his straw hat from the pressures of the world. Although Paul has disclaimed any ambition, he nevertheless feels that he is somebody special. To wish he were stupid is already to have acknowledged that he is intelligent and different. And though he is protesting that he wants to be a part of his community and to be normal, Paul is also saying that to be normal is to be stupid, unconscious like an animal or like a working man. Even as he feels the attraction of community, "the beloved home valley," his metaphors betray his underlying repugnance for the working class.

Lawrence "cheats about the story of his adolescence" by abstracting Paul's drive to become an individual from a social context; he treats his conviction of superiority and his desire to develop himself as something different from the social ambitions of his mother, Miriam, Clara, and William. The social formations and institutions which foster the desire for independence and identity, part of the background from which Paul emerges, drop from sight in the second half of the novel, when sex replaces society as the arena in which one develops. The story of how Lawrence left the Midlands becomes the story of how Paul left his mother; Paul is represented as the passive victim of women who channel their frustrated social ambitions through him. Finding his identity in sexual revolt against these women, he discovers in sex an alternative to upward mobility and a potential resolution of the dilemma of becoming someone—a distinct, superior someone—without leaving home.

*   *   *

Two short stories, composed while Lawrence was working on the first draft of "Paul Morel," reveal the "suppressed secret" of his ambition and even his snobbery; both indicate that upward mobility complicated his maturation and his relationships with women. As early considerations of Lawrence's relationship with Jessie Chambers, "A Modern Lover" and "The Soiled Rose" (later revised as "The Shades of Spring") shed light on the development of Paul and Miriam.

The protagonists of both stories are readily identifiable portraits of the author; each has spent several years in London and at the opening of the tale is returning to a Haggs Farm setting and a reunion with a past love. Each is conscious of a painful degree of social distance between himself and the people to whom he is returning. In "A Modern Lover," when Cyril Mersham sits down to dinner with his old friends, he finds he is

> extremely attentive to the others at table, and to his own manner of eating. He used English that was exquisitely accurate, pronounced with the Southern accent.... His nicety contrasted the more with their rough, country habit. They became shy and awkward, fumbling for something to say... he felt how irrevocably he was removing them from him, though he had loved them.[9]

The stories offer a considerably more ironic view of the protagonist than we get in *Sons and Lovers*. Not only have Mersham and Syson caused the rupture in the relationship with the "Miriam" figure by leaving her, but they are also guilty of stringing her along, tantalizing her with their intellectual powers and luring her away from a local rival. Although the protagonist's sexual prowess is seriously questioned in both stories, his power over the woman's imagination is reaffirmed.

In "A Modern Lover" Cyril Mersham has come down from London to see if his old sweetheart will become his lover. As his name punningly indicates, he is a "mere sham" in several ways. Posturing as a city man, he assumes a southern accent with her family and pretends to a citified ignorance of the country with his rival Vickers simply for his own amusement. On the other hand, he tells Muriel that he has come to her "from the south . . . because—well, with you I can be just as I feel . . . without being afraid to be myself" (ML, 20), which suggests that he may feel like a "sham" in the city too. Pressing Muriel to have sex with him, Cyril assures her that he would like to marry her (though his debts prevent him) and that she need not worry about getting pregnant. (Presumably the modern lover is equipped with modern contraceptives.) The couple's exchange is similar to one in *Sons and Lovers* in which Paul pressures Miriam (283), and in both fictions the woman hears the man's reassurance that there is no danger "in the Gretchen way" as a clear signal that he does not want to risk commitment or responsibility; hence she is understandably reluctant to accept a lover who merely poses as a future husband.

Cyril is a "sham" in offering himself as a lover not only because he does not want to make a commitment but also because he seems to be more stimulated by intellectual than physical interchange. He scoffs at Vickers, whom he characterizes as "an old-fashioned, inarticulate lover; such as has been found the brief joy and the unending disappointment of a woman's life." He easily outshines his rival in Muriel's eyes by talking well "of art and philosophy— abstract things that she loved, of which only he had ever spoken to her. . . ." But seeing Vickers bent over his bicycle Cyril thinks: "After all . . . he's very beautiful; she's a fool to give him up. . . . She could have some glorious hours with this man—yet she'd rather have me, because I can make her sad and set her wondering." Later as he walks in the fields with Muriel, Cyril "playfully" suggests that she should choose Vickers in preference to himself, for he [Cyril] cannot love "blindly" and in fact must pull his "flowers to pieces, and find how they pollinate, and where are the ovaries" (ML, 20). This analytical approach extinguishes ecstasy, "but [the flowers] mean more to you; they are intimate," he says.

When Muriel hesitates to have sex, her lover is considerably cooled. "It was as if she had tipped over the fine vessel that held the wine of his desire, and had emptied him of all his vitality. He had played a difficult, deeply-moving part all night, and now the lights suddenly switched out, and there was only weariness." Though Muriel tries to rouse him from "coldness," he has "lost hold—for to-night" (ML, 22). In the parallel scene in *Sons and Lovers,* Paul's sincerity and steadiness are far less critically questioned, and the emphasis falls on Miriam's timidity and sexual disgust. Her lover is not unmanned, and she resolves to force herself to "submit, religiously, to the sacrifice" (284). The problem between Lawrence and Jessie Chambers was certainly more than one of social distance, and the novel probes their relationship with insight and complexity, but it places the failure of their physical relationship on Miriam's shoulders and does not relate her timidity to her lover's unreliability or to the problems created by his departure for the city. In their final breakup Paul says, "I can't help that it's failed," and Miriam responds, "It has failed because you want something else" (298). In the context of the novel the "something else" is the all-important physical relationship, but the short story suggests that the man wants that and a good deal more: social mobility and his new, intellectual life in London.

Cyril is responsible for cultivating Muriel's tastes, indeed, for pushing her into mental consciousness.

> He had fiercely educated [her] into womanhood along with his own struggling towards a manhood of independent outlook. They had breathed the same air of thought . . . they had expanded together in days of pure poetry. . . . [He] lifted Muriel as in a net, like a sea-maiden out of the waters, and placed her in his arms, to breathe his thin, rare atmosphere. (ML, ll, 17)

Muriel tells Cyril that he brings her and her family "to a certain point, and when you go away, we lose it all again"; although she says that this is not his fault, he is responsible again that evening for raising her aspiration beyond Tom Vickers and then walking out on her. In "The Shades of Spring" Hilda accuses Syson of a similarly callous, analytical attitude to their relationship. "You plucked a thing and looked at it till you had found out all you wanted to know about it, then you threw it away" (SS, 207). But to her charge that he has discarded her, Syson responds:

> Yet it was you who sent me the way I have gone. . . . You *would* have me take the Grammar School scholarship. . . . You wanted me to rise in the world. And all the time you were sending me away from you—every new success of mine put a separation between us, and more for you than for me. You never wanted to come with me: you wanted just to send me to see what it was like. I believe you even wanted me to marry a lady. You wanted to triumph over society in me. . . . I distinguished myself to satisfy you. (SS, 208)

This argument is used again in *Sons and Lovers:* pushing men "to rise in the world," women use them to realize their own ambitions; the man's betrayal in leaving is then shifted on to the woman. Women, not men, are responsible for the separation and are to blame for the protagonist's feeling of estrangement.

"The Shades of Spring" neatly reverses the characters of Paul and Miriam. Syson recognizes belatedly that he has always failed to appreciate Hilda's physical nature.[10] Like Cyril he has pushed his sweetheart into mental consciousness. Hilda complains: "You were always making me to be not myself.... You took me away from myself.... I am like a plant ... I can grow only in my own soil" (SS, 206–8), much as Paul complains to Miriam. Through her relationship with a gamekeeper Hilda discovers that "It is one's self that matters ... whether one is being one's own self and serving one's own God" and that "one is free" through sex. She discovers, too, the Lawrencian idea of impersonality. "The man doesn't matter so much" (SS, 205), she says, as Paul says of Clara.

Through a physical relationship with a lower-class character, both Hilda and Paul recover their "freedom" from an overly intellectual or spiritual companion and discover their own self-sufficiency, but neither is content to remain in and grow with this sexual relationship. In the novel Paul leaves Clara because he is dominated by his love for his mother, but Hilda's dissatisfaction has a social dimension. She recognizes that her gamekeeper-lover is "inventive, and thoughtful—but not beyond a certain point." When Syson inquires where the keeper "comes short," she says: "The stars aren't the same with him.... You could make them flash and quiver, and the forget-me-nots come up at me like phosphorescence. You could make things *wonderful*" (SS, 207). When Muriel asks Cyril "Why do women like you so?" he responds: "Because I can make them believe that black is green or purple—which it is, in reality" (ML, 15). Both short stories acknowledge the power of words (and of education) which makes the intellectual protagonist more appealing than the inarticulate but physically satisfying lover. In the end Hilda refuses, just yet, to marry the gamekeeper: something more than sex is needed for genuine fulfillment.

Traits which are shared by the protagonist and the woman in the two short stories are firmly segregated in the novel. Syson, like Miriam, is an idealizer who can never be more than a spectator of passion. He prefers to see Hilda in literary or religious terms: a nun, a Botticelli angel, a Beatrice to his Dante. At the end of the story he views his own alienation in literary terms, as he lies in the grass, watching Hilda and her keeper, like a knight in a William Morris poem, "lying always as dead, and yet did not die." Both Syson and Mersham are destructively analytical: they pluck flowers and tear them apart in order to know them and then cast them aside, an action which suggests much about how they approach sex. They enjoy intellectual stimulation; seeing Hilda, Syson feels "the old, delicious sublimation, the thinning, almost the vaporising of himself, as if his spirit were to be liberated" (SS, 203). The reference to rarified air recalls the passage in which Cyril lifts Muriel out of the water "to breathe his thin, rare atmosphere." In *Sons and Lovers* it is Miriam who lifts Paul into this breathless zone when she shows him her white roses (160).

In the novel this mental consciousness belongs only to Miriam: the habit of viewing the world through a book, the abstract or analytical approach which kills what it seeks to know, the sublimation of sexuality in intellectual exchange. These are, in effect, the charges against her which make it necessary for Paul to leave her. Paul, however, retains the engaging variability of Cyril and Syson, the verbal dexterity which makes the natural world seem "wonderful." Yet Paul has little of their snobbery, their effete lethargy, or their putative ambition; he does not suffer from the alienating effects of education and mobility. He combines the gamekeeper-rival with the intellectual far-traveler, achieving independence through sexual experience which gives him a consciousness of his "own self and [his] own God."

The endings of the short stories and the novel are strikingly similar. In each case the enervated protagonist summons his determination to leave the woman and heads toward the city. However, in the two stories the geographical distinction between city and country, between south and north, is an analogue for the social distance which neither couple can overcome, even though neither partner is fully satisfied with one class or locale. The protagonist's decision to return to the city represents a break with his class and past and his commitment to an ongoing intellectual life. Mersham and Syson are unquestionably pained by this choice. In *Sons and Lovers,* however, Lawrence avoids this sense of choice: Paul *must* grow up by breaking the tie with his mother. The fact that his "release" comes only with her death underlines his radical passivity in the matter of his own development. Because the geographical and social oppositions have not been developed in the novel, we are not conscious that Paul is making a break with his community when he walks quickly "towards the faintly humming, glowing town." Although his mother is dead, Paul, we feel, has not really lost anything; on the contrary, he is "released" into life. He chooses to be instead of not-to-be, but he does not have the hard choice of what kind of self to be. He even accomplishes the longed-for union with his mother because, by turning towards the city, he "carr[ies] forward her living, and what she had done ... her effort" (412).

*   *   *

The short stories, of course, are not better or more truthful than the novel. But they do suggest that Lawrence's mobility was a factor in his relationship with Jessie Chambers which is "suppressed," to use Pritchett's word, in *Sons and Lovers.* One result is that Miriam is blamed for the failure of her relationship with Paul. Or at any rate he is excused; for if sex is the key to self-development and identity, Paul has no choice but to turn away from Miriam and to reject their mutual intellectual development as an unhealthy substitution of books for bodies.[11]

The scene in which Paul teaches Miriam algebra illustrates the tension between the complexity of Lawrence's material and his need to fit it to a thesis. The tutoring project is initiated because Miriam is frustrated with the role which sex and class have prescribed for her.

> "I want to do something. I want a chance like anybody else. Why should I, because I'm a girl, be kept at home and not allowed to be anything? What chance *have* I?"
>
> "Chance of what?" [Paul asks.]
>
> "Of knowing anything—of learning, of doing anything.... Why *should* it be that I know nothing?"
>
> "What! such as mathematics and French?"
>
> "Why shouldn't I know mathematics?" (154)

Her exasperation puzzles Paul, who is presumably free from such ambition, but he is willing to share the fruits of his schooling, which mean little to him. The next evening Miriam is anxious, reluctant to begin the lesson, and so to delay she brings in "some big greenish apples" for Paul. They then work together over the book until he becomes irritated by her proximity and speaks sharply to her about her slowness in learning. As their lessons continue, Paul cannot keep his temper, and at one point he throws a pencil at her. "And because of the intensity to which she roused him, he sought her" (157). How much Lawrence includes in this scene: Miriam's resentment of her lot along with her understandable reluctance to test herself; the blend of sexual and intellectual interest which she and Paul find in each other; the way the frustration of the superior, quick student, embarrassed at Miriam's "humility" before him, shades into the irritation of sublimated desire; the fact that Paul seeks her out because of several kinds of intensity to which she rouses him. Their relationship has variety and complexity in Lawrence's dramatic presentation; however, within the context of the novel, the scene acquires a particular emphasis. Miriam is Eve, tempting Paul to share with her the apple of knowledge; though apparently his student, she is controlling him, forcing him to channel his sexuality into mental activity, and this provokes his hostility. The complex matter of a young man and woman's mutual development along several fronts is subordinated to the overriding argument that genuine development occurs only through the sexual relationship, which affords the son a way of establishing his identity apart from his mother.

The suppressed issue of Lawrence's rise also affects Paul's relationship with Clara and helps to explain why he treats her somewhat contemptuously. Like Miriam and Mrs. Morel, Clara is ambitious and frustrated. Although married to a working-class man, through the women's emancipation movement "she had acquired a fair amount of education, and having some of Miriam's passion to be instructed, had taught herself French" (264). Her low-status job at Jordan's, offering no scope for her intelligence, bores her; again like Miriam and Mrs. Morel, she strikes others as "superior," "Queen Clara" who puts on airs. And yet Clara is shown to be completely satisfied by her sexual relationship with Paul. For Paul, too, their sex is deeply gratifying, but he soon becomes annoyed by her demands. He explains to his mother: "I don't care what her opinion of me is. She's fearfully in love with me, but it's not very deep. . . . Sometimes, when I see her just as the woman, I love her . . . but when she talks and criticises, I often don't listen to her" (350).

Paul's experience of sex with Clara is similar to Hilda's in "The Shades of Spring"; it gives both of them "everything"—specifically the natural world and a sense of identity—but it is an impersonal sex in which "the man [or woman] doesn't matter very much." Hilda's lover is her intellectual and social inferior, and although she has gained something through him, she cannot be contented with a world which excludes Syson's intelligence and imagination, the very qualities which have taken him far from her. Quite unreasonably Paul also regards Clara as his inferior. On one of their last walks, Paul reflects that "even if they married . . . still he would have to leave [Clara], go on alone . . . each [of them] wanted a mate to go side by side with" (316). Then he turns to Clara and says, laughing: "But we walk side by side, and yet I'm in London arguing with an imaginary Orpen; and where are you?" (361). Sir William Orpen was one of the most successful artists of the day; one has to wonder why this young clerk at Jordan's should think that his imagined conversations make him superior to a co-worker equally self-educated.

In reality Lawrence had moved socially and geographically beyond the women who contributed to the composite character of Clara: Louie Burrows, Alice Dax, and perhaps some of his women friends at Croydon. By 1910 he had a teaching degree and a job in London; he had attracted some notice as a promising writer and was enjoying an expanding circle of acquaintances. These wider horizons are implicit in Paul's casual remark about being in London arguing with Orpen but not developed in the novel. Lawrence's sexual and intellectual maturation, his growth in self-confidence, his certainty about his future as an artist, the clear sense that "he would have to leave" not only "Miriam" and "Clara," but Eastwood and Nottingham—all this comes to Paul without any change in his social estate, almost without any change in his friends, and crucially, without any conscious effort on his part.

When Paul disposes of Clara by handing her back to the humbled Baxter Dawes, Lawrence registers no sense of injustice or unfitness. In the course of ten years, through a social movement, Clara has grown beyond her class, though she has not been able to find work to suit her abilities except as a speech-making suffragette. She is at the end of the novel very much in Mrs. Morel's position in the opening, but nothing alerts us to this parallel. Clara "deserves" Baxter since she, along with the other women in the novel, stands accused of wanting to "possess" her man. Paul tells her: "I consider you treated

Baxter rottenly. . . . You made up your mind he was a lily of the valley and it was no good his being a cow-parsnip. You wouldn't have it . . . love should give a sense of freedom, not of prison" (360). Apparently it is up to Clara to limit herself to Baxter's horizons but fine for Paul to put her and Miriam behind him, on the grounds that "love should give a sense of freedom." Inexplicably, he is able to go to London and have that imagined conversation with Orpen, though he has actually done less than Clara in the novel to realize that freedom.

In contrast to the three other protagonists of this study, Paul does not suffer major setbacks nor does he have to shed any illusions about himself. What he learns from his relationship with Miriam is not that he has failed her, or she him, but that "it had always been a failure between them" (291). Nor does he take any responsibility for his relationship with Clara; she quietly becomes part of his past. Sex for Paul has none of the ineluctable consequences, both social and biological, that it has for Jude, Clayhanger, and Peak. In each of the three earlier novels, the protagonist's conflict in his personal, sexual life is bound up with his social existence; his character as lover has no independent existence. Paul is free, as they are not, of the guilt of trying to break with the past and with his class, of the responsibility of trying to expand the self beyond the given social limits, of the burden of past mistakes which would cripple him for the future. This freedom is effected by suppressing the social dimension of Paul's maturation and by tailoring the story of his development to Lawrence's thesis about maternal possessiveness.

*　　*　　*

Sons and Lovers shuns the social double bind of upward mobility only to face a psychological double bind. For the story of oedipal attachment does not so much replace the story of upward mobility as repeat its problematic in a different register. Paul's development is made difficult by his sense of being possessed by his mother, created by her, driven and harried by her needs and desires, trapped in a smothering union with her and, contradictorily, pressed by her to push upward into an alienating, mechanical world. The story of oedipal attachment is intimately related to the story of upward mobility, for it is mother who both dreams of individuation and pushes her sons up and away in order to realize that dream. Paul turns to sex as a weapon to use against the woman who had appropriated his being and forced him into mental consciousness. He thus brings an aggressive edge to the sexual relationship in his urgent need to protect his individuality. At the same time he finds in sex a way of achieving the independence and individuality which his mother valued, a way superior to upward mobility since it requires no separation from "the beloved home valley" and no compromise with the vile industrial civilization. The issue, then, in the sexual arena is the same as in the social: how to achieve individuation while maintaining relatedness. Although there would be moments of balance, ultimately Lawrence was as unable to imagine a resolution of the sexual double bind as he was to find in his life a resolution to his deracination.[12]

When Paul is only six, he watches his mother ironing:

> [Her] mouth closed tight from suffering and disillusion and self-denial . . . she looked brave and rich with life, but as if she had been done out of her rights. It hurt the boy keenly, this feeling about her that she had never had her life's fulfilment: and his own incapability to make up to her hurt him with a sense of impotence, yet made him patiently dogged inside. It was his childish aim. (66)

To say merely that Paul has an oedipal complex is not enough. At this young age he is aware that his mother's life has been cramped and unfulfilled. He wants to compensate her for this deprivation, and because her requital can come only through her children's success in a social structure which has deprived her, Paul's life is consecrated to realizing her ambitions for him. In expanding himself, he is always working for her; the greater his success, the greater the bond between them. Similarly Miriam's participation in his intellectual and artistic development binds her to him and yet creates in him the sense that he is not his own man. Both women demand that he discipline himself either through the regimented work at Jordan's or through the sexual repression which Miriam enforces in the name of spiritual love.

Mrs. Morel's possessiveness toward her sons is as much a matter of thwarted social ambitions as of sexual frustration.

> Now she had two sons in the world. She could think of two places, great centres of industry, and feel that she had put a man into each of them, that these men would work out what *she* wanted; they were derived from her, they were of her, and their works also would be hers. (101, Lawrence's emphasis)

Later, of Paul alone:

> She had a great belief in him, the more because *he was unaware of his own powers.* There was so much to come out of him. Life for her was rich with promise. She was *to see herself fulfilled.* Not for nothing had been *her* struggle. (183, emphasis added)

As each boy is encouraged to enter the world of trade, the world beyond and above the Bestwood collieries, he is doing "what *she* wanted." She appropriates their commercial and artistic successes, the fruits of "her struggle." Paul in particular is like a hand puppet, "unaware of his own powers" and thus moved by her ambitions.

Her sexual possessiveness always has a social dimension. When William writes home about his "Gipsy," she sees him "saddled with an elegant and expensive wife, earning little money, dragging along and getting draggled in some small, ugly house in a suburb." It is difficult not to take this at face value, the legitimate concern of a mother who knows what the effect of an early marriage will be on her son's career and what personal unhappiness can come from frustrated ambition. From what we see of Gipsy, her fears are warranted; even William shares them: "You know, mother... Gyp's shallow. Nothing goes deep with her" (133). Both Paul and William adopt their mother's standard of education and cultivation, and this puts them between classes; although they disdain the women of Bestwood and are not fooled by a veneer of purchased elegance, they are intimidated by women who are their social superiors. Gertrude Morel's aspirations for Paul are explicit: she "frankly *wanted* him to climb into the middle classes, a thing not very difficult, she knew. And she wanted him in the end to marry a lady." While Paul is still torn between Miriam and Clara, "she wished he would fall in love with one of the girls in a better station in life. But he was stupid, and would refuse to love or even to admire a girl much, just because she was his social superior" (257). Mrs. Morel's ambition and their own class-consciousness are major factors in undermining her sons' relationships with their sweethearts.

In the final version of the novel, Lawrence intended William's death to show the fatal power of the mother's love and her hold over her sons. He had written his editor Edward Garnett that his novel was about a mother who

> selects [her sons] as lovers—first the eldest, then the second. These sons are *urged* into life by their reciprocal love of their mother.... As soon as the young men come into contact with women, there's a split. William gives his sex to a fribble, and his mother holds his soul. But the split kills him, because he doesn't know where he is.

As Delavenay notes, Lawrence's exclusively psychological explanation does not take into account the following passage about William's deracination.[13]

> There seemed to come a kind of fever into the young man's letters. He was unsettled by all the change, he did not stand firm on his own feet, but seemed to spin rather giddily on the quick current of the new life. His mother was anxious for him. She could feel him losing himself. (90)

The exhausting experience of social dislocation added to his sexual frustration eventually wears William out. Delavenay surmises that William is partially a projection of Lawrence and that Gipsy may owe something to one of Lawrence's London girlfriends. To support this interpretation, I would add that William's rapid social rise in London really belongs to Lawrence. "[William] was soon visiting and staying in the houses of men who, in Bestwood, would have looked down on the unapproachable bank manager and ... the Rector.... He was, indeed, rather surprised at the ease with which he became a gentleman" (90). As a clerk earning £120 in an underwriters' firm, William is not likely to have risen so far so fast, but Lawrence, because of his writing, was visiting with F. M. Hueffer and Violet Hunt and staying with the Garnetts by 1910. William's experience reflects Lawrence's ambition, anxiety, excitement, and loneliness and reveals something of the grim struggle of the unclassed man to gain a footing in London. His death combines the fact of Lawrence's brother's death in 1892 with Lawrence's bout of pneumonia in 1911 after three years of pronounced social deracination. William's fate is a grim warning—perhaps even an accusation—about ambitious as well as sexually possessive mothers, and it suggests that Lawrence found the personal cost of upward mobility very high indeed.

Mrs. Morel's jealousy of Miriam and her relative acceptance of Clara is best explained in terms of her own frustrated social situation, which in turn affects her psychological relationship with Paul. She wants to be the sole force behind her son's ambition so that his success will be hers. When his painting wins a prize, his mother cries, "Hurrah, my boy! I knew we should do it!" (253). She wants that "we" to be Paul and herself alone. His success alone can redeem her life. She thinks:

> . . . the life beyond offered very little. . . . She saw that our chance for doing is here, and doing counted with her. Paul was going to prove that she had been right; he was going to make a man whom nothing should shift off his feet; he was going to alter the face of the earth in some way which mattered . . . her soul stood by him, ready as it were, to hand him his tools. She could not bear it when he was with Miriam. (222)

Paul is going to make up for her husband and her own impotence by being independent and powerful enough to affect the world. She alone will give him the wherewithal to succeed (will "hand him his tools"), and precisely because she can give him so little materially, she values those intangibles she offers as his standards and his inspiration. No wonder she resents Miriam who also stimulates Paul's hunger for a richer world.

In the early scenes at Willey Farm, Paul responds positively to a new, "spiritual" dimension embodied in Mrs. Leivers and Miriam. The circuit of stimulation on this spiritual or mental plane is clearly fruitful for his painting. Miriam encourages him to articulate his intentions, and his "sayings . . . gave her a feeling of life again, and vivified things which had meant nothing to her. She managed to find some meaning in his struggling, abstract speeches. And they were the medium through which she came distinctly at her beloved objects" (152). But Paul resents being a "medium" for her as for his mother. Both women use him as an avenue through which to realize their own ambitions. He is a literal Christ figure for Miriam (171), a worldly redeemer for his mother, even though both women believe that they are sacrificing themselves to him.

Sex is Paul's way of rebelling against his mother's and Miriam's possessiveness, against their puritanical values, against their demand for sublimation in the name of education and self-cultivation. Hence Paul's relationship with Clara is both aggressive and regressive. It helps to establish his separation from Miriam and his mother and to heal the split between mind and body which they have demanded; but sex with Clara is also a way of possessing the mother and of recovering the lost unity with her after she had thrust him into the world of mental abstraction and industrial mechanization. The real mother had sent William off to London and had taken Paul to Jordan's, but in the substitute mother, Clara, Paul is reunited with the natural world. His rejection of Clara may also serve as a way of punishing his mother, denying her ambition and returning her to the working-class man of whom she has demanded too much.

Paul hopes to establish his identity through sexual experience, but he finds that sex is fraught with the dangers of union, merger, and loss of self. After he consummates his relationship with Miriam, he feels obliterated.

> [H]e felt as if nothing mattered, as if his living were smeared away into the beyond.... To him now, life seemed a shadow, day a white shadow; night, and death, and stillness, and inaction, this seemed like *being*. To be alive, to be urgent and insistent—that was *not-to-be*. The highest of all was to melt out into the darkness and sway there, identified with the great Being. (287)

Sex offers escape from the "urgent and insistent" pressures on his daylight self—pressures to rise socially—but here, at least, this is accompanied by a dangerously seductive release from the responsibility of individuation.

His encounters with Clara seem at first to afford a positive expansion of being. She is "life wild at the source staring into his life, stranger to him, yet meeting him.... They had met, and included in their meeting the thrust of the manifold grass stems, the cry of the peewit, the wheel of the stars" (353). Though exhilarating, this expansion into "nothingness" and "impersonality" also threatens identity. Clara is said to have "gained *herself*, and stood now distinct and complete" (361), but Paul feels "imprisoned when she [is] there, as if he could not get a free deep breath, as if there were something on top of him" (359). Paul's rejection of Clara is an indication of his mother's hold on him, but it is not just a sexual hold. He shares her values, her desire for self-development, her ambition, and her yearning for the city as a center of culture. Because of this he finds his sexual relationship with Clara inadequate. He returns to his mother, and when, at the close of the novel, Paul turns toward the city, he faces once again his peculiar dilemma of "carry[ing] forward her living" by becoming himself.

*   *   *

Lawrence's marriage to Frieda von Richthofen would have half-satisfied and half-shocked his mother, exactly the combination which he needed. It seemed as well to provide a magical resolution to the dislocation of the unclassed man. Union with a foreign aristocrat, with her healthy contempt for the British bourgeoisie, allowed Lawrence to feel that he had escaped the limiting environment of the Midlands working class without accepting a place in the middle class. It also encouraged him to put his faith in private solutions to complex social questions. In his imagination, marriage overwhelmed the role played by talent, ambition, a liberalized educational system, and those social formations within the petty bourgeoisie which fostered his independence and self-worth. Lawrence never dramatizes the struggle of a youth developing within society, in the teeth of a given social order. We do not see his characters struggling to wrest an identity distinct from the omnipresent "social molds." They are always heading for Taos or Italy or Birkin's vague "somewhere," preserving an illusory freedom, assuring us that there is a self that can be realized apart from material or social conditions and apart from history.

If before 1912 Lawrence sought for ways to avoid taking full responsibility for his social advance, with Frieda he needed more than ever to deny that the individual is responsible for his actions. Their union suggested a rationale—but it had a telltale contradiction. The individual is brought into being by a force far beyond his control. This life force, sexual passion, takes the power of shaping his destiny out of the individual's hands, so that he is no longer personally responsible, yet it gives him the power to realize a self. The logical impasse demands the creation of "another ego," which will assume the burden of preserving its individuality, its "firm singleness" vis-à-vis a woman. To have a self, yet not to be responsible for it, to have separate identity and union simultaneously: these are the crucial contradictions which Lawrence would struggle to resolve.

In a letter of June 1914, he describes his new concept of character to Edward Garnett.

> ...somehow—that which is physic—non-human, in humanity, is more interesting to me than the old-fashioned human element—which causes one to conceive a character in a certain moral scheme and make him consistent.... I don't so much care about what the woman *feels*—in the ordinary usage of the word. That presumes an *ego* to feel with. I only care about what the woman *is*—what she *is*—inhumanly, physiologically, materially... what she *is* as a phenomenon...instead of what she feels according to the human conception.... You mustn't look in my novel for the old stable ego of the character. There is another ego, according to whose action the individual is unrecognisable....[14]

Delavenay suggests that Lawrence's theory of the unconscious, which he began to elaborate in the fall of 1912 after he and Frieda had left England together, was a way of rationalizing the act of running off with another man's wife.[15] The elevation of the instinctual blood consciousness and the denigration of the merely social self, "the old stable ego" drawn in "a certain moral framework," are part of the continuing process of self-justification. The conception of "another ego" allowed Lawrence to deny responsibility not just for running off with another man's wife but for breaking away from Eastwood, Nottingham, and the working class and for creating himself as a separate individual. He preferred to think of the developmental process as beyond his control and to disclaim any role in his own alienation.

Like Paul Morel, Ursula Brangwen in *The Rainbow* is attempting to become a self. To show her achieving her individuation and her eventual separation from her community guiltlessly, Lawrence needed his theory of "another ego." The self should be passive, its development not "willed" but accomplished through a "drive-to-being." In *Study of Thomas Hardy* (1914) he likens this drive to the natural force urging a seed into the light to become the "poppy-self." He invokes another natural force in the following passage from *The Rainbow*. Ursula is leaving her village of Cossethay for college. The neighbors speak to her in a thick Midlands dialect which "demanded of her in the old voice the old response."

> And something in her must respond and belong to people who knew her [but] she was ashamed because she did feel different from the people she had lived amongst. It hurt her that she could not be at her ease with them any more. And yet—and yet—one's kite will rise on the wind as far as ever one has string to let it go. It tugs and tugs and will go, and one is glad the further it goes, even if everybody else is nasty about it. (419)

Self-development does not come through specific acts for which the individual is responsible: "Not I, not I, but the wind that blows through me."[16]

Using these botanical metaphors for self-development and his theory of "another ego," Lawrence transforms the *social* superiority which Paul and Ursula feel in their "old stable egos" into an unexamined, unchallenged, inherent conviction of their inner superiority. That social superiority is evident in Ursula's attitude to the people of Cossethay. From childhood on, she wants to build barriers between herself and the common Billy Pillenses; she views Grammar School as "a great release...from the belittling circumstances of life" (263) and the obligatory association with vulgar neighbors. "What right have I to be poor?" she demands (285). This powerful sense of her own superiority is intimately tied to her desire "to become a self-responsible person" (334). Her studies give her a sense of exhilaration and liberation, and her success at school feeds her self-confidence and opens the way to pupil-teaching, scholarships, and eventually college—the way Lawrence took up and out of Eastwood.

However, Lawrence represents Ursula's upward mobility as a false avenue for development. Her efforts to gain social independence and some external recognition of her superior status are misguided; they bring disillusionment but no serious compromise of herself, for her real development must take place at the deeper level of "another ego," or as she calls it "her Sunday self." Although she can do nothing to "will" the other ego into being, the fact that she is capable of this unconscious development is the mark of her genuine superiority. At the end of the novel Ursula retreats to Beldover to await the Prince Charming who will recognize this superiority and sweep her off to Europe, sparing her the tiresome and painful process of developing within a social context. It's true that the endings of Lawrence's Bildungsromane are tentative, and the sexual relationships which would assuage his protagonists' loneliness without threatening their identity remain elusive. But at the end of the novels Paul and Ursula are both released from an encounter with death to stand at the threshold of a new life. Living mysteriously isolated within a community they disdain, their primary commitment to self-realization seems to be affirmed, and nothing suggests that we should view their hopefulness with irony or see in their attitude of proud aloofness a barrier to the sense of relationship which they seek.

*   *   *

Arnold Kettle describes the central theme of *The Rainbow* as "the attempt to express and hence resolve the paradox that each human being is at once separate and yet a part of a whole, independent yet interdependent, a lone individual yet a social being."[17] *The Rainbow* opens with a description of the Brangwen farmers who are intimately connected to the cycle of seasons and to the fertility of the earth, who have "lived for generations on the Marsh Farm." As in *Sons and Lovers,* aspiration and ambition are associated with women.

> The women were different... they looked out from the heated, blind intercourse of farm-life, to the spoken world beyond.... The woman wanted... something that was not blood-intimacy. She stood to see the far-off world of cities and governments and the active scope of man.... She faced outwards... to discover what was beyond, to enlarge their own scope and range and freedom....
>
> What was it in the vicar that raised him above the common men?... It was not money nor power nor position.... She decided it was a question of knowledge....
>
> It was this, this education, this higher form of being, that the mother wished to give to her children. (8–10)

Although the life of "blood-intimacy" is richly rendered, both men and women want wider horizons, an experience of what is foreign and other, a finer individuation of themselves to be gained through knowledge. The rainbow is a symbol of the connection between earth and human aspiration, a promise that the individual can develop himself and achieve a "higher form of being" without losing the intimate relationship which the men share with the natural world.

Tom and Lydia are thoroughly realized in the context of a particular social and natural landscape, and in their marriage they achieve a balance between physical connection and mental expansion, between individuation and union, between Flesh and Word, as Lawrence puts it in *Study of Thomas Hardy*. Their social existence is part of this reconciliation, represented by the rainbow. By the end of the novel the oppositions have changed: the need to come to terms with the social world and with mental consciousness is denied. The concern for social integration which will permit growth of the individual is replaced with the concern for psychic integration, for in the psyche alone the individual is free to develop—or so Lawrence seems to say. Farm and city, which provide the context in which the individual must work out his destiny, are forsaken for a psychic landscape symbolized by the earth, mud, darkness, light and fire, images which grow out of but no longer refer to a social reality. Although Lawrence struggles to make Ursula's rainbow vision at the end coherent with the earlier sections of the novel, he does not succeed in connecting her psychic integration with the social world.

The argument of *The Rainbow* is that in industrial civilization mental consciousness has triumphed: man, hard-shelled and egoistic, has lost his sense of interrelatedness to all living things. Hence the need to return to values associated with the "blood-intimacy" of the Brangwen men. Along the way Lawrence loses sight of the original objective: achieving individuation in an expanded social world. The result is that it does not matter who Ursula *is* in a social sense: whether she is foreign or provincial, educated or ignorant, upper-middle or working class, financially independent or in the poorhouse—none of this matters, supposedly, when she meets one of the "Sons of men."

In *The Rainbow* Lawrence explores the inner, psychological world of men and women in ways that no other author had attempted; such pioneering art enriches our understanding of human beings. But the new interest in the psychic life and the new techniques of rendering the unconscious did not *require* him to dismiss the social world. The first five chapters provide ample evidence that Lawrence could show the social world impinging on his characters' unconscious life. The first third of the novel is superior to the rest precisely because Lawrence is not limited by a static, "inhuman," "physiological," or "material" conception of character as a "phenomenon" apart from social life.

The chapters on Anna and Will probably reflect some of the storminess as well as the sexual satisfaction of Lawrence's early life with Frieda; here his fear that man would be engulfed by woman surfaces, and his interest becomes more exclusively psychological, the social context vaguer and less relevant. Will, the craftsman who is inarticulate, has a good deal in common with Walter Morel, and both are hounded and criticized by wives who have a strong sense of their own superiority, who wish their men were more ambitious, less willing to merge their identity with the community of the pub, in Morel's case, or with the religious ecstacy of the church in Will's. Anna Victrix is overweening in her sexual pride, conquering the husband who is faulted for his failure to "come into being," before she lapses into the quiescence of motherhood. Their story alerts us to the dangers of sexuality: merger and loss of self-definition.

In contrast to both her parents, Ursula feels the Brangwens need to realize her "complete nature" in the "finer, more vivid circle of life." "Out of the nothingness and the undifferentiated mass, to make something of herself!... How to act, that was the question? Whither to go, how to become oneself?" (283–84). Her desire "to become a self-responsible person" and her "all-containing will... for complete social independence" from her family reflect Lawrence's own concern to get out of Eastwood and to develop himself. Grammar School allows Ursula "to burst the narrow boundary of Cossethay, where only limited people lived" (264). She craves "some spirituality and stateliness" which she finds in her studies, and these seem to offer the genuine inner expansion which the original Brangwen woman sought in education.

> [Ursula] trembled like a postulant when she wrote the Greek alphabet for the first time.... A Latin verb was virgin soil to her: it meant something, though she did not know what it meant. But she gathered it up: it was significant. When she knew that: $x^2 - y^2 = (x + y)(x - y)$ then she felt that she had grasped something, that she was liberated into an intoxicating air, rare and unconditioned.... In all these things there was the sound of a bugle to her heart, exhilarating, summoning her to perfect places.... (269)

While she is still in school, her desire for independence is stimulated by the example of Winifred Inger; through her and her Uncle Tom, Ursula confronts the industrial world which turns humans into machines. In Wiggiston she has a vision of a life of "homogeneous amorphous sterility," "disintegrated," "mechanical," "inchoate," "a moment of chaos perpetuated... chaos fixed and rigid" (345–46). The images for the factory town stress alternately its fixed and amorphous character, either extreme a threat to the individuality Lawrence is seeking.

Ursula turns her back on this civilization to pursue her independence by becoming a pupil-teacher; but the St. Philip's School is a "prison," another instance of the life-denying character of the modern world. Eventually Ursula leaves for Nottingham University College, where learning proves conclusively to be a dead end, a false rainbow, an arc of light which circumscribes too little of experience. She attempts to explore the dark world beyond this light with Skrebensky, but he, like Winifred Inger and Tom Brangwen, is associated with modern industrial civilization in which social identity has become a hard shell, a substitute for a living self.

Oppositions conceived with complexity early in the novel are simplified in the course of Ursula's development. In the opening pages the world of culture, associated with the female, the city, mental vitality, freedom and individuality was balanced with the world of nature, associated with the male, the farm, physical vitality, and constraint of the individual. But as a Brangwen woman entering "A Man's World," Ursula encounters only sterility, rigidity, and deadness. This encourages her to retreat from culture to nature and to discover there an expansion of being, a freedom, and a complex interiority opposed to the urban, daylight world of mental activity. Though linked in imagery, this inner world remains separate from both the material reality of the farm and the social reality of working-class Cossethay.

Judged by the values of darkness which Ursula discovers at the end of the novel, her education contributes nothing to the essential development of her "other" ego. In theory, her school-teaching, like her relationships with Winifred and Skrebensky, shows only the corruption of modern society and justifies Ursula's rejection of the social world and her inward-turning. But in fact the detailed realism of these chapters on her pupil-teaching and her college experience make a convincing "vale of soul-making." In them Ursula is a living, complex character, more interesting than the comparatively "inhuman" and "physiological" "phenomenon" which she appears to be in the sex scenes.

At seventeen, restless and dependent upon her parents, neither of whom were "quite personal, quite defined as individuals" (353), Ursula determines to win her independence, her freedom, and her self. She writes to the mistress of the High School who advises her to become a teacher.

> "I cannot tell you how deeply I sympathise with you in your desire to do something. You will learn that mankind is a great body of which you are one useful member, you will take your own place at the great task which humanity is trying to fulfil....
>
> If only you could learn patience and self-discipline, I do not see why you should not make a good teacher....
>
> I shall be proud to see one of my girls win her own economical independence, which means so much more than it seems. I shall be glad indeed to know that one more of my girls has provided for herself the means of freedom to choose for herself."
>
> It all sounded grim and desperate. Ursula rather hated it. (358)

Rather than attacking this abstract idealism directly, as he does in "First Love" and in "Shame," Lawrence allows the schoolmistress's prim tone to suggest the limitations of her ideal and to justify Ursula's reaction. It does sound "grim and desperate," but she goes to the library anyway to copy out ads for teaching positions. Like Paul Morel "she shrank with extreme sensitiveness and shyness from new contact, new situations.... The whole thing was so cruel, so impersonal. Yet it must be done." When she posts her applications, "she felt as if already she was out of the reach of her father and mother, as if she had connected herself with the outer, greater world of activity, the man-made world" (361). These last phrases, putting Ursula in the line of Brangwen women, beautifully combine the aspiration of chapter 1 with an echo of the schoolmistress's language. This dialogic narrative voice incorporates both irony and idealism, showing the dialectical tension between individual aspiration and the inevitably limiting social molds in which it may be realized. As long as both aspects are registered, Lawrence works his theme at its fullest complexity; but often in *The Rainbow* he ends the dialectical struggle by denying the conflict: the individual simply removes herself to nature, opting out of the social world.[18]

Once she gets a job, Ursula finds that the schoolroom changes her character.

> The prison was round her now! ... She was here in this hard, stark reality—*reality*. It was queer that she should call this the reality, which she had never known till to-day ... and Cossethay, her beloved, beautiful, well-known Cossethay ... that was minor reality.... It was queer to feel that one ought to alter one's personality. She was nobody, there was no reality in herself, the reality was all outside of her, and she must apply herself to it. (372-73)

From the standpoint of his philosophizing, Lawrence would have us believe that Ursula has got it all wrong here, that the project of school-teaching is an act of "her cold will" rather than of her living self. But in this chapter he renders actual experience with such honesty and psychological insight that he makes us feel how Ursula grows under shocks of change which violate her hopes and ideals. The schoolroom *is* a prison, yet within it Ursula expands her horizons, her opportunities, and her knowledge of herself. Her intention to be "so personal" and to establish a "vivid relationship" with her students is thwarted by the reality of "fifty-five reluctant children" who must be compelled "into one disciplined, mechanical set" if minimal learning is to go on. Ursula is a romantic dreamer, and reality is radically flawed, but by submitting herself to the conflict between the two she matures. On her first payday, when Ursula gives her mother fifty shillings for board, we share in the triumph of her newly won independence even as we acknowledge the limits of this gesture of petty defiance. She has won so much and so little. "She had another self, another responsibility. She was no longer Ursula Brangwen, daughter of William Brangwen." Of course, she is and she isn't. She feels free but also "could not escape.... It was a case now of being Standard Five teacher, and nothing else" (390).

Ursula "lived in the ignominious position of an upper servant hated by the master above and the class beneath." We are reminded of Jane Eyre and the long history of frustrations of those who through education have found themselves caught between classes. Grim as this school-prison is, Ursula finds here a measure of independence and self-knowledge. Experience teaches her the truth of the schoolmistress's prim asseveration that self-development needs self-discipline. "It was always a prison to her, the school. But it was a prison where her wild, chaotic soul could become hard and independent" (407). And this prison opens the door to college.

Elsewhere Lawrence suggests that Ursula has another out—a way of escaping the difficult negotiation of oppositions. Feeling trapped in her studies, Ursula thinks:

> ...she knew that she had always her price of ransom—her femaleness. She was always a woman, and what she could not get because she was a human being, fellow to the rest of mankind, she would get because she was a female.... In her femaleness she felt a secret riches, a reserve, she had always the price of freedom. (334)

(Imagine what Charlotte Brontë would say to that!) If Lawrence is aware of the irony of using the language of the market ("price of freedom") to get out of the marketplace (into the freedom of marriage?), then it is an irony he drops when his oppositions become simplified: when woman is no longer associated with culture and mental activity but with nature and undifferentiated flesh. Indicating that Ursula's whole effort to develop her female self in "a man's world" is a misguided project, he allows her a magical escape when she runs off to Europe with Birkin.

From her grammar school days, Ursula is puzzled by the duality of the "Sunday world" and the "weekday world." "The Sunday world was not real, or at least, not actual. And one lived by action. Only the weekday world mattered," she thinks; one had to be responsible to oneself within the weekday world. Yet "[t]here was some puzzling, tormenting residue of the Sunday world within her, some persistent Sunday self, which insisted upon a relationship with the now shed-away vision world" (284). Lawrence returns to this dichotomy in "A Man's World" when Ursula and her fellow teacher Maggie Schofield discuss "life and ideas" over tea.

> Maggie was a great suffragette, trusting in the vote. To Ursula the vote was never a reality. She had within her the strange, passionate knowledge of religion and living far transcending the limits of the automatic system that contained the vote. But her fundamental, organic knowledge had as yet to take form and rise to utterance... the liberty of woman meant something real and deep. She felt that somewhere, in something, she was not free.... She was in revolt. For once she were free she could get somewhere... the somewhere that she felt deep, deep inside her.
>
> In coming out and earning her own living she had made a strong, cruel move towards freeing herself. But having more freedom she only became more profoundly aware of the big want.... (406)

Through this and the next two chapters, the value of making the self in the "weekday world" is undermined by these hints of an entirely different "reality" which Ursula is presently missing. The theoretical dualism of Sunday-weekday belies the dialectical complexity of life in which social experience is integrated with private and even unconscious experience. In the realistic presentation of a wretched school system, we do not feel that the weekday world is without value or that Ursula is failing to be "responsible to [her] self" in struggling with it. Quite the contrary.

The passage continues: "She wanted so many things. She wanted to read great, beautiful books, and be rich with them; she wanted to see beautiful things...to know big, free people; and there remained always the want she could put no name to." Does the social freedom of a job and further education create the conditions for recognizing "the big want"? That is, does objective freedom create the desire and conditions for subjective freedom? Or is social freedom simply a false avenue, an exposure to the emptiness and negation of social life? Lawrence does not answer the question definitively here, but we know where his emphasis lies. Even though the chapter as a whole convincingly dramatizes the role of the social world in shaping Ursula, Lawrence postulates a separate, inner world of the Sunday self, in which "the strange, passionate knowledge of religion and living" (the phrasing is bound to remind us of the inchoate, undeveloped Will Brangwen, whose very limitations Ursula is seeking to escape) is said to "far transcend" the mechanical, social world, which includes "the automatic system" of the vote and St. Philip's School.

The "fundamental, organic knowledge" of the Sunday self has yet to take "form" or "utterance" but evidently exists apart from and even prior to social experience. It is not brought into being through social experience. Ursula's sense that she is both free and not-free, which is perfectly understandable in the social context of the school, is now mystified, and the complex tension of being free and caught is reduced to the simpler idea that "somewhere, in something, she was not free." Her unclassed social situation, in which she must serve those above and beneath, leads to an inner "revolt," a desire for release into "the wonderful, real somewhere that was beyond her, the somewhere that she felt deep, deep, inside her." What is socially "beyond" (the world of books, art, and "big, free people" who appreciate them) is now located within Ursula and spoken of in religious-sexual terms. The rhetoric of "deep, deep inside her" reduces the complexity of Ursula's desires to a craving for a transcendent sexual satisfaction which will give her both "the beyond" and herself.

Jude, Clayhanger, and even Peak desire social mobility in order to bring the "beyond" world "inside" themselves, to make freedom mean something "real and deep." But Hardy, Bennett, and Gissing, by consistently relating such inward development to social experience, raise hard issues which Lawrence evades: specifically the role of class and education in self-cultivation. They look critically at the romantic ideals and the inner conviction of superiority of their protagonists and probe the interaction between subjective and objective worlds; their critique of society is generated by the clash between the protagonist's ideals and ambitions and an actual social situation in which he attempts to realize them. When in *The Rainbow* Lawrence attempts a similar consideration of the relation between social mobility and individual development, he treats Ursula's effort to *will* her self-development ironically because, in his mythology, her whole project is misconceived. Her disillusionment at college, which we might compare with Jude's experience at Christminster, turns out not to matter particularly; disappointment with the world simply redirects her to her Sunday self, her true self, her other ego. Her clash with reality is not a tragedy but a victory—because she can escape into the true arena for self-cultivation. The conflict between the self and society is dissipated, with the result that we do not feel so keenly as in *Jude the Obscure* the anguish about what the social world can do to the individual.

*   *   *

The final three chapters of *The Rainbow* explore Ursula's estrangement from her childhood world. Before she goes off to college, her family moves to Beldover where, because of her father's new position, they will be "among the elite. They would represent culture" (422). The move gives Ursula no end of satisfaction. "After all, it is better to be princess in Beldover than a vulgar nobody in the country." Their new home provides all the family with "a delightful sense of space and liberation, space and light and air." In his detailed description, Lawrence suggests how the social rise creates new possibilities for inner development, the soul taking nourishment from factors which seem so uneconomic—space and light and air. These are part of "the widening circle" even though they supposedly have nothing to do with "the big want."

As in *Sons and Lovers,* Lawrence moves from a detailed presentation of a social milieu and of a family's effort to distinguish itself from the rest of the working community even by slight social signals, to his insistence upon his protagonist's unquestioned inner superiority, which is no longer a matter of class but of psychic development. He asserts the inevitability of a break between this individual and the community. As Paul has no choice but to leave Miriam and Clara, so Ursula's friendship with Maggie Schofield simply begins "to drift apart, as Ursula broke from that form of life wherein Maggie must remain enclosed" (412). No reason is given for the difference in their careers, except for our general sense that Ursula is a magically superior person and not so foolish as Maggie to trust in the vote to achieve freedom. Her latent snobbishness is evident in the account of her rejection of Maggie's brother Anthony, a gardener who, like Hilda's gamekeeper-lover in "The Shades of

Spring" is in some way unsatisfying for an educated woman. Ursula is attracted to the satyr-like natural man, but finds him "ridiculous" dressed up in Sunday clothes trying to impress her. When he proposes, she feels she is "in the grip of some insult." The power of his attraction is strong, and it is only with difficulty that she rejects him. Although the tug of the natural world is great, there is no question that Ursula is right to say no.

> She turned away . . . and saw the east flushed strangely rose, the moon coming yellow and lovely upon a rosy sky. . . . All this so beautiful, all this so lovely! He did not see it. He was one with it. But she saw it, and was one with it. Her seeing separated them infinitely. (416)

The scene explicitly confirms her decision to go on to college: "All her life . . . she returned to the thought of him. . . . But she was a traveller . . . on the face of the earth, and he was an isolated creature living in the fulfilment of his own senses." Anthony can offer her only the mindless "blood-intimacy" of the Brangwen men who fail to "see" what they are a part of. Like the Brangwen woman, Ursula has no intention of staying among the "obscure laborers" who like Anthony are "isolated creature[s] living in the fulfilment of [their] senses." The last phrase reveals the underlying contempt, rooted in class feeling, which she has for the laboring man; it implicitly acknowledges the superiority of her mental effort to achieve something more than sensual gratification. In embryo this relationship mirrors Paul's with Clara, only here the reasons for breaking it off are explicitly related to class and intellectual ambition.

Anthony Schofield, Anton Skrebensky: laborer and aristocrat—neither lover offers Ursula what she wants. Her plight is similar to Connie's in *The First Lady Chatterley* where she is torn between the impotent but articulate Clifford and the sullen proletarian Parkin. But in *The Rainbow* as in *Lady Chatterley's Lover* the issue of class is muted, the role of social mobility in individual development played down, and the need for mental consciousness well-nigh obscured.

Ursula is disillusioned by college which she perceives as an irrelevant adjunct to industrial society, "a little apprentice-shop where one was further equipped for making money" (435). Her true self cannot be developed here but only in the darkness: "That which she was, positively, was dark and unrevealed, it could not come forth. It was like a seed buried. . . . " The world of college is "like a circle lighted by a lamp," which she had mistakenly taken to include all the world. "Yet all the time, within the darkness she had been aware of points of light, like the eyes of wild beasts, gleaming, penetrating, vanishing. And her soul had acknowledged in a great heave of terror only the outer darkness" (437). That Ursula must explore this darkness she knows only because she has arrived at a certain level of consciousness which "infinitely separates" her from Anthony Schofield. In the sterile classroom, she has a vision which speaks to her Sunday self. Her botany professor argues that there is no "special mystery to life [which is merely] a complexity of physical and chemical activities." But looking through the microscope at a cell, Ursula sees "the gleam of its nucleus" and ponders its purpose.

> It intended to be itself. But what self? Suddenly in her mind the world gleamed strangely... she only knew that it was not limited mechanical energy, nor mere purpose of self-preservation.... It was a consummation, a being infinite. Self was a oneness with the infinite. To be oneself was a supreme, gleaming triumph of infinity. (441)

This insight speaks to Ursula's earlier sense that oneself is "merely a half-stated question" and to her need to bring that self into being, not for a purpose *beyond* itself, but for the pure purpose of self-realization. Such an ideal is not necessarily anti-social; one can see Lawrence working between the extremes of Spencerian individualism ("mere... self-preservation and self-assertion") and the mindless collectivism of Skrebensky. The problem is that by analogizing the human being with a cell, seed, or flower, Lawrence denies the self a conscious role in determining its being. He reduces Ursula, the perceiver, to what is perceived, and as a model for human relations he replaces the mechanical laws of the industrial world with "the strange laws of the vegetable world" (436).[19] What is omitted, from now on in Lawrence's fiction, is the project of *becoming* a self. One does not develop: one *is*. The very conditions which permit Ursula to reflect upon herself (the daylight world of the laboratory, the educational system, the desire to rise) are spurned by her "stronger self that knew the darkness" (452).

Exploring that darkness through her sexual relationship with Skrebensky, she becomes "strangely free, strong... as if she had received another nature. She belonged to the eternal, changeless place.... Her soul was sure and indifferent of the opinion of the world of artificial light." This is a wholesale rejection of weekday reality, "artificial light," and social being in favor of an inner, "permanent self" which exists in darkness, with an almost belligerent emphasis on the independence of this self even from the sexual partner who had swept her away "into the pristine darkness of paradise." She rejects Skrebensky and the empty social role of "young wife of a titled husband on the eve of departure for India" (454).

When Ursula discovers that she is pregnant and writes to Skrebensky to say that, after all, she will accept that role, her unconscious bursts upon her in her vision of horses. She becomes aware of a bedrock self which lies "like a stone, unconscious, unchanging, unchangeable... at rest on the bed of the stream, inalterable and passive, sunk to the bottom of all change" (490). Her "isolated, impregnable core of reality" challenges "the ache of unreality, of her belonging to Skrebensky" or to her father and mother, or to Beldover,

Nottingham, England or "this world." "They none of them exist, I am trammelled and entangled in them, but they are all unreal. I must break out of it, like a nut from its shell which is an unreality." Finally Lawrence returns to the image of a seed: Ursula is "the naked, clear kernel thrusting forth the clear, powerful shoot," and the rest of the world is "all husk and shell." "She had her root in new ground," he claims, though we haven't the least idea where that ground might be. Discovering her "other ego"—a "permanent self" existing in darkness—could not be more explicitly linked to a rejection of the social world, which is why when we move directly into her rainbow vision, the rhetoric rings so hollow. In her story, especially with her conviction of superiority which is, despite Lawrence's intentions, so obviously fostered by her upward mobility, there is nothing to convince us that the "sordid" colliers on whom she gazes do have "arched in their blood" the rainbow of human aspiration which depends upon light. The metaphor of their germination is false to the story of Ursula's struggle into individuality. These closing images deny the truth of the first pages that a sense of interiority is enhanced by social conditions: by knowledge and education.

At the end of *The Rainbow,* Ursula, like Paul, has achieved individuation through sexual experience but not a sexual relationship; she has not achieved that balance between nature and culture, farm and city, private and social, unconscious and conscious which Tom and Lydia have in their relationship, and which is signified by their rainbow. Instead, Lawrence denigrates the world of "light" and stresses sex as a way of bringing into being "another ego" in which the private, conscious self is not connected to the social world but to the impersonal, undifferentiated world of nature and the unconscious: "the eternal fields of darkness" to which Skrebensky takes her, the darkness of the horses of her unconscious, of the stream where she lies like a stone under water, of the earth in which she germinates. The "other ego," which comes into being independently of an individual's will, leaves him connected with the permanent universe, "the carbon," and also separated out into "diamond"—to use the images from Lawrence's letter of June 5, 1914.[20] The emphasis on blood consciousness at the expense of mental consciousness provides a way of knowing which does not involve the eye and the mind, a way of resolving the apparent contradiction of "seeing and being one with," a superior way of knowing which leaves Ursula "infinitely separate" from Schofield but imaginatively connected to his world of darkness.

*   *   *

Lawrence is a passionate critic of bourgeois civilization. In celebrating "the whole man alive" he opposes ideas which legitimate the class structure—the superiority of mind over the body, the virtue of repression. At his best the celebration of individuality shows him the falsity of any social stratification.

> Where each thing is unique in itself, there can be no comparison made. One man is neither equal nor unequal to another man. When I stand in the presence of another man, and I am my own pure self, am I aware of the presence of an equal, or of an inferior, or of a superior? I am not. . . . I am only aware of a Presence, and of the strange reality of Otherness. There is me, and there is another being.[21]

Lawrence's theories about sex and blood consciousness are an attempt to reconcile contradictions which originate in the social structure, to accommodate middle-class individualism and working-class communalism. But as the social oppositions are translated into private "polly-analytics," an elitist element persistently emerges. Arguing that sex is the only way to achieve a sharply defined self, he makes this definition the basis for social discriminations. The developed continue to be at the top of a hierarchy, the unrealized beneath them; these include both the unconscious laboring people, whom Lawrence had risen above, and most of the class to which he has risen, who have moved too far from the life of the body. Ultimately his theory of blood consciousness provides Lawrence with a symbolic way of belonging to the working class while remaining "infinitely separate" from it.

This aspect of Lawrence informs his 1918 essay "Education of the People" in which he argues for a hierarchical, authoritarian schooling system which replaces education with social conditioning save for all but a select few.[22] The saddening irony of this essay is not just that Lawrence attacks the very system which contributed to his own escape from limiting social circumstances, but that he wants to perpetuate a social hierarchy based on the kind of interior development which is a product of education. The mark of his new elite will be this interiority, produced by education, and it will then be in the power of this elite to deny such development to the masses. In this essay and in the novels of this period, *Aaron's Rod, Kangaroo,* and *The Plumed Serpent,* the potentially democratic stress on the uniqueness of the individual self, incomparable to any other, gives way to the assertion that some beings are nettles and some are luxurious blooms; from this follows a social hierarchy in which the individual has no freedom to develop. The botanical metaphor of self-as-flower, just like the theory of "another ego," removes from the individual any control over and any responsibility for his development and destiny. Having climbed out of the working class, Lawrence kicked over the ladder he had used and denied the role which ambition and social mobility had played in his own development.

Lawrence's critique of industrial society is marred by his deep-seated ambivalence about class; by his refusal to value the historical changes wrought by bourgeois institutions in his own life and in society; and by a persistent emphasis on a private, fantastic resolution modelled on his own experience. For all his loathing of bourgeois civilization, Lawrence wanted to preserve social classes in order to maintain his own distinction from the working class. Thus he took his revolution inward, offering an experience of liberation and an expansion of the self through sex but not in the crucial areas of education, politics, or economy.

Conclusion

This study has proposed that literary forms have ideological content and that formal and thematic innovations may reflect disruptions in that informing ideology. The case in point is the English Bildungsroman which initially articulated the values and interests of a rising middle class, linking the full, harmonious development of the individual to his upward mobility. The genre smoothed out the contradiction between affirming a traditional social hierarchy and supporting the individualism which would be disruptive of that order. In the course of the nineteenth century, this fundamentally comic Bildungsroman moved in the direction of moral fable, satire, and tragedy, registering in these shifts increasing doubts about the liberal ideology it had been so well-suited to articulating.

Amid the general disillusionment with bourgeois society by the century's end, the writers in this study constitute a special case. For them the initial promise of the Bildungsroman was compelling. Coming from the petty bourgeoisie, they needed to avail themselves of new opportunities for mobility to move up into the middle class. But by rising they became part of a social transformation which in many respects they deplored. They confronted in an immediate way the contradiction between the individual's right to develop and the social consequences when that right is extended to the many. Following Arnold, they felt that in the new order of Barbarians, Philistines, and Populace, the traditional standard of culture which hitherto had justified movement up the social hierarchy had become eroded. Doubting whether their own advancement would be culturally or personally enriching, they also resented the inevitable association with an entire class of upwardly mobile, "pushing" entrepreneurs. In their lives they seemed to resolve these tensions by becoming citizens of Arnold's unclassed republic of letters, but in their novels they exposed the elusiveness of that ideal.

The protagonists of their Bildungsromane are economically vulnerable youths, uncertain about their aspiration and talent, and under no illusions that the provincial world of their childhood offers an alternative to the effort to escape. The result is the double bind situation explored in these chapters in which the protagonist's attempts to develop are all thwarted. To advance socially is to be tainted by vulgar, self-serving ambition, but failure to advance means that one's potential is certain to be stunted. The dream of the harmonious expansion of the self in a society which nurtures it becomes a nightmare of estrangement and loss of self. Those painful experiences which, in earlier novels, might have led to maturation here contribute to disintegration: "Experience *un*teaches."

It is the task of bourgeois ideology to make us see ourselves "as free, unified, autonomous, self-generating individuals; and unless we did so we would be incapable of playing our parts in social life."[1] As anti-Bildungsromane, *Born in Exile* and *Jude the Obscure* treat this conception of the individual as a yearned-for ideal which cannot be realized. Jude ends in "a chaos of principles—groping in the dark," and Peak comes to experience a "tormenting metaphysical doubt of his own identity." What is taken to be the fin de siècle pessimism of Gissing and Hardy is grounded in their profoundly disruptive experience of deracination. They detect that there is "something wrong somewhere in [the] social formulas" if talented individuals can be so frustrated, and both protagonists rebel against the class structure. But as we have seen, this rebellion is abortive and the social system remains intact after their death. What makes both novels so very bleak is that the values implied in the protagonist's challenge to the status quo are denied, even as the values of the status quo are exposed as empty.

Such pessimism is of course substantially moderated, for different reasons, in the novels of Bennett and Lawrence. Edwin Clayhanger is able to effect an accommodation with the provincial world, and it is a delicate matter to estimate the value of that compromise. Bennett is intermittently aware of the dignity and beauty of the human spirit struggling to express itself through, rather than in spite of, the ordinary; such awareness challenges the privileged world of culture which ratifies the class structure. But ultimately he turns from this alternative to affirm that reconciliation by which Edwin finds his home within a sterile, upper-middle class world. Lawrence, by contrast, emphatically rejects both bourgeois and proletarian communities, envisioning his protagonist's escape from social molds through sexual experience. However, he transposes into this ostensibly private arena the fundamental conflict he experienced within the class structure: namely, the need for individuation and relatedness, the need to climb up without leaving home.

In his novel *Kipps,* H. G. Wells captures the disruptive effects of this social deracination.

All the way up and all the way down the scale there's the same discontent. No one is quite sure where they stand, and everyone's fretting. The herd's uneasy and feverish. All the old tradition goes or has gone, and there's no one to make a new tradition. Where are your nobles now? Where are your gentlemen? They vanished directly the peasant found out he wasn't happy and ceased to be a peasant. There's big men and little men mixed up together, that's all. None of us know where we are. Your cads in a bank holiday train and your cads on a two thousand pound motor; except for a difference in scale, there's not a pin to choose between them. Your smart society is as low and vulgar and uncomfortable for a balanced soul as a gin palace, no more and no less; there's no place or level of honour or fine living left in the world; so what's the good of climbing?

Wells offers in this novel a comic exploration of the same double bind experienced by Gissing, Hardy, Bennett, and Lawrence. His lower-middle class draper's apprentice is catapulted into genteel circles by a surprise inheritance, there to be patronized, humiliated, manipulated, and exasperated until in disgust he retreats to the shop-keeping world in which he feels at home. The scene in which Kipps dines in the Royal Grand Hotel while sitting uncomfortably on his hat and experiencing great difficulty with his fork is a wonderfully liberating version of that painful luncheon during which Peak experiences his double consciousness. The fact that Wells feels free to laugh and to make us laugh suggests that he has achieved some necessary distance on the dilemma faced by the other authors.

Certainly he perceived the problem in political rather than personal terms. The contradictions which our other novelists had registered in the individual's sense of inadequacy or projected as metaphysical disorder are shown by Wells to have their origin in a social and political context. Kipps's discomfiture is occasioned by an anachronistic class structure. The pointlessness of upward mobility is captured succinctly: "All the old tradition . . . has gone . . . so what's the good of climbing?" As soon as the peasant resents the gentleman's advantages, the ancient distinction between classes is revealed as a sordid standoff between "big men" and "little men," between haves and have-nots, which demands a political response. The passage is spoken by the socialist Masterman who calls for redistribution of property, public housing, and good state education.[2] However, Kipps ignores this potentially collectivist alternative to the class structure and retreats to his comfortable nook in the lower-middle class, content to enjoy a share of the material prosperity of Edwardian England, while Masterman's projected role in Book III is radically cut. Wells would develop his political views in his next work, *A Modern Utopia,* where we can see him take the same turn as Lawrence did in the 1920s. Disenchanted with bourgeois capitalism, neither author is able to put any faith in collective action or in social democracy; they recreate the class structure in their idea of a new leadership, which will govern the masses and arrange their affairs. Wells's Samurai, like Lawrence's mystical power figures, are latter-day versions of Arnold's "aliens," members of an unclassed elite whose role is to preserve a standard of culture to which the mass remains insensible. While Wells and Lawrence escape the double bind by rejecting the existing class structure, their imaginations remain bound by a concern shared by the other authors of this study—namely, the desire to find the talented individual a privileged home apart from the masses.

Notes

Introduction

1. The most valuable study of the German tradition is Martin Swales's *The German Bildungsroman from Wieland to Hesse* (Princeton: Princeton University Press, 1978). Marianne Hirsch's article "The Novel of Formation as Genre: Between Great Expectations and Lost Illusions" in *Genre,* 12 (Fall 1979), 293–311, provides a valuable comparative study of the German, French, and English traditions of Bildungsroman and a helpful seven-point definition of the genre. Against the position that the only true Bildungsroman is a German Bildungsroman, Hirsch argues for a European "novel of formation," carefully distinguishing the more optimistic, politically conservative German variant from the English and French "novels of disillusion" so well analyzed by Harry Levin and Georg Lukács. Jerome H. Buckley's *Season of Youth: The Bildungsroman from Dickens to Golding* (Cambridge: Harvard University Press, 1974) stresses thematic features such as the move from country to city and the ennobling versus the debasing love affairs; the autobiographical involvement of the author; and the interest in the psychological formation of the character. G. B. Tennyson provides a helpful definition of the term in his "The Bildungsroman in Nineteenth-Century English Literature," in *Medieval Epic to the 'Epic Theater' of Brecht,* R. P. Armato and J. M. Spalek, eds. (Los Angeles: University of California Press, 1968), 135–46. My initial assumptions about the new middle-class reading public depend upon the magisterial work of Ian P. Watt, *The Rise of the Novel* (Berkeley: University of California Press, 1965).

2. G. Robert Stange, "Introduction" to W. M. Thackeray's *The History of Henry Esmond, Esq.* (New York: Holt, Rinehart, and Winston, 1962), xx.

3. In *Myths of Power: A Marxist Study of the Brontës* (New York: Barnes and Noble, 1975), Terry Eagleton suggests that Charlotte Brontë's fiction is an attempt to fuse two sets of values associated with the gentry and the rising industrial bourgeoisie: culture, tradition, conservatism, and the habits of piety and submission must be reconciled with rationality, shrewd self-seeking, energetic individualism, radical protest, and rebellion. Her heroines develop through their struggle to accommodate both sets of values.

4. See Peter Smith's valuable discussion of the complications which Estella poses in the ending of *Great Expectations* in his *Public and Private Value: Studies in the Nineteenth-Century Novel* (Cambridge: Cambridge University Press, 1984).

   Unlike Dickens, George Eliot refuses to separate the moral development of her characters from their material and social situation. For her, as for Hardy, the intellect is ambitious, the emotions conservative, so that either upward mobility or stasis threatens the development of the whole person. The ending of *The Mill on the Floss* suggests that this conflict is irresolvable. Eliot is the first major writer to face the particular problems of the aspiring petty bourgeoisie, but because she was "unclassed" not only by virtue of her social background but also by her sex and later her relationship with G. H. Lewes, I have not sought in her work the preoccupations and motifs common to the four male authors included in this study. I exclude George Meredith as well because, while his own social position was ambiguous, he felt from early on a comfortable identification with the upper-middle class.

5. The term "double bind" has been given clinical precision by Gregory Bateson. In his 1955 presentation of the relationship between double bind experiences and schizophrenia, he alludes to the general use of the term; it is this nonclinical concept which I use. Bateson said: "By [double bind] I mean a sequence of experiences such that when [a person] solves a problem of human relationship at the level at which it is apparently offered, he will find himself in the wrong at some other level. To solve the problem within a given area *ipso facto* means to have unsolved it in terms of some other area." Quoted by Milton M. Berger, M. D. in his "Introduction" (xv) to *Beyond the Double Bind: Communication and Family Systems, Theories, and Techniques with Schizophrenics* (New York: Brunner/ Mazel, 1978). Bateson speaks of "a problem of human relationship," by which, in his clinical work, he means a relationship between two individuals, usually parent and child, within the context of the nuclear family. Social structures, however, are also "human relationships," and it seems reasonable to extend the concept of double bind to include situations in which one hears an injunction at one level—say, to succeed in life according to criteria offered by a hegemonic class—which is contradicted at another level by a second injunction—say, to be true to oneself. If that "self" is felt to belong to, or to have been shaped by experiences within a subordinate class, then an individual might feel himself in a double bind, able to obey one injunction only by violating the other.

6. Raymond Williams comments on this change in his discussion of the term "class" in his *Keywords: A Vocabulary of Culture and Society* (New York: Oxford University Press, 1976), 51–59.

> The essential history of the introduction of *class*, as a word which would supersede older names for social divisions, relates to the increasing consciousness that social position is made rather than merely inherited. All the older words, with their essential metaphors of standing, stepping and arranging in rows, belong to a society in which position was determined by birth. Individual mobility could be seen as movement from one *estate, degree, order* or *rank* to another. What was changing consciousness was not only increased individual mobility, but the new sense of a SOCIETY . . . or a particular social system which actually created social divisions, including new kinds of division.

7. The quotation is from Brian Simon's *Studies in the History of Education: 1780-1870* (London: Lawrence & Wishart, 1969), 366.

Both the Clarendon and Taunton Commissions proposed three grades of schools, distinguished by the classes which would patronize them: "lower middle-class, middle middle-class, and higher middle-class." The first grade was for students who aimed at the university and was intended to serve "the upper-middle and professional classes; first, those with large unearned incomes, successful professional men, and business men 'whose profits put them on the same level,' second, the clergy, doctors, lawyers, and the poorer gentry, who 'have nothing to look to but education to keep their sons on a high social level.'" A second grade was for those leaving school at sixteen. "They would prepare for the army, the medical and legal professions, the civil service, civil engineering, business and commercial life; and, it was envisioned, would be patronised largely by the mercantile and trading classes—larger shopkeepers, rising men of business, substantial tenant farmers. Since, the Commissioners felt, some of these 'are not insensible to the value of culture in itself, nor to the advantage of sharing the education of the cultivated classes,' Latin might be included in the curriculum, though not Greek." The third grade was for those leaving school at fourteen, the sons of "smaller tenant farmers, small tradesmen and superior artisans. . . . Education for boys of this class was to be strictly limited; none must be permitted to stay beyond the age of fourteen, or the school would tend to encroach on the work of schools of the grade above." Simon, 323–24.

8. Simon, 298.

9. Simon writes about the Clarendon Commission established in 1864 to propose reforms for nine public schools that "their overriding concern [was] to establish an exclusive upper-class system of education; one which could stretch to include the sons of wealthy industrialists and professional men, but which must at all costs be kept free from the encroachments of tradesmen and the lower orders beneath." Simon, 312. A major recommendation was to ignore founders' provisions for poor scholars, transferring scholarship monies to the middle class.

10. Lawrence Stone, "Literacy and Education in England: 1640–1900," in *Past and Present*, 42 (Feb. 1969), 72. See also his "The Size and Composition of the Oxford Student Body: 1580–1909," in *The University in Society, Vol I: Oxford and Cambridge from the Fourteenth to the Early Nineteenth Century*, Lawrence Stone, ed. (Princeton: Princeton University Press, 1974) for confirmation of Simon's assertions about the exclusiveness of the universities in the late-nineteenth century.

11. Stone, "Literacy," 72.

12. Quoted in Simon, 356.

13. Simon, 335.

14. From *Culture and Anarchy*, in *The Complete Prose Works of Matthew Arnold*, vol. 5, R. H. Super, ed. (Ann Arbor: University of Michigan Press, 1965), 90 and 95.

15. The term "aliens" is from *Culture and Anarchy*, 146; the idea of the "saving remnant" is elaborated in Arnold's essay "Numbers; or the Majority and the Remnant" in *The Complete Prose Works*, vol. 10, 143–74.

16. Arnold's use of the term "unclassed" occurs in "The Incompatibles" in *Complete Prose Works*, vol. 9, 241. "Now there are insignificant people, detached from classes and parties and their great movements, people unclassed and unconsidered, but who yet are lovers of their country, and lovers of the humane life and of civilisation. . . . "

17. Compare Eagleton's discussion of Arnold's importance in *Criticism and Ideology: A Study in Marxist Literary Theory* (London: New Left Books, 1978), 102–10.

18. V. S. Pritchett, *The Living Novel and Later Appreciations* (New York: Random House, 1964), 155.

19. My definition of "ideology" is taken from Louis Althusser, "Ideology and Ideological State Apparatuses" in *Lenin and Philosophy* (London: New Left Books, 1971). The ensuing paragraph is indebted to Terry Eagleton, *Criticism and Ideology*, in particular his discussion of Pierre Macherey's concept of "de-centering" in "Towards a Science of the Text," and to Fredric Jameson, *The Political Unconscious*, especially "On Interpretation: Literature as a Socially Symbolic Act."

Chapter 1

1. For my perspective on Gissing's early novels I am indebted to Fredric Jameson, "Authentic *Ressentiment:* The 'Experimental' Novels of Gissing," *Nineteenth-Century Fiction,* 31, no. 2 (Sept. 1976), 149. This essay appears in revised form in *The Political Unconscious: Narrative as a Socially Symbolic Act* (Ithaca: Cornell University Press, 1981). Like Jameson, Alan Swingewood argues that Gissing's thesis novels are aimed at demonstrating the inalterability of the social structure: in *The Novel and Revolution* (London: Macmillan, 1975), 124–30.

2. The standard biography is Jacob Korg's *George Gissing: A Critical Biography* (Seattle: University of Washington Press, 1963). Gillian Tindall's *The Born Exile* (New York: Harcourt, 1974) is particularly good on Gissing's experience at Owens, stressing that his act was specifically a working-class crime "utterly out of keeping with the class with which the whole Gissing household fervently wished to be associated.... he had blundered back through those very social barriers which, by dint of work and scholarships, he had himself so laboriously climbed. No wonder that he was to feel after that he had somehow given the game away about himself—that he had betrayed an essential looseness in his nature, and, at the same time, that if he were to keep this secret trait carefully concealed in future, he would be guilty of a lack of integrity..." (130). Tindall here identifies another double bind related to and exacerbating Gissing's anxieties about class. John Halperin's *Gissing: A Life in Books* (New York: Oxford University Press, 1982) provides some further biographical details.

3. The passage is quoted by Raymond Williams in *Culture and Society: 1780–1950* (New York: Harper & Row, 1958), 176. Williams uses the term "negative identification" to describe that process by which an adolescent rebel or outcast "finds available to him an apparent cause, on behalf of the outcast of society, in a mood of rebellion." Disillusion generally follows, as in Gissing's case.

4. Quoted by Jacob Korg in his "The Spiritual Theme of 'Born in Exile,'" in *Collected Articles on George Gissing,* Pierre Coustillas, ed. (New York: Barnes and Noble, 1968), 136, and in his *George Gissing: A Critical Biography,* 167. Pierre Coustillas notes: "The narrative contains innumerable echoes from actual life; a detailed analysis of them would amount to a study of Gissing's creative methods, of the mental alchemy through which the data supplied by memory, observation and imagination were fused into the fully realized people and events of the story." From his "Introduction" to *Born in Exile* (Sussex: Harvester Press, 1978), xi. Subsequent references to this edition will appear in parentheses in the text.

5. Lionel Trilling, *Sincerity and Authenticity* (Cambridge: Harvard University Press, 1971), 43. Subsequent quotations from this text are taken from 37, 38, and 43.

6. Jameson, 145. "...*blank irony,* a state in which judgment is called for but indefinitely withheld."

7. Two recent studies single out this chapter, praising Gissing's psychological portrait of Peak's "double consciousness" which makes his deception more complicated than simple hypocrisy. The fullest discussion is Adrian Poole's in *Gissing in Context* (Totowa, NJ: Rowman and Littlefield, 1975), 164–75. Robert L. Selig takes special note of this material in his *George Gissing* (Boston: G. K. Hall, 1983), 67–71. The best critical studies of *Born in Exile* are Poole's and John Goode's in *George Gissing: Ideology and Fiction* (New York: Harper and Row, 1979).

8. "*Foris ut moris, intus ut libet*" (194): Outside as custom would have it; inside as it pleases you.
   In his partial chapter on *Born in Exile,* John Goode develops a perspective on the novel similiar to my own but formulated in more abstract, Marxist-sociological terms. Goode

focuses on the "linked problematic of intellectual emancipation and social mobility," which takes a peculiar form in late-nineteenth-century England. Here the "organic intellectual" that Peak might have been (indeed, probably would have been in France or Russia) is pulled strongly toward the role of the "traditional intellectual," with strong identification with an outdated landed aristocrisy. Peak is

> the traditional intellectual, educated by capitalist money, conscious of bourgeois science thrust into a world whose ideology is still 'aristocratic'—the more so as the bourgeoisie itself becomes more and more populated with *rentiers* whose lifestyle necessarily resembles that of the 'gentry,' and whose privilege depends not on the 'free' thought of bourgeois ideology but on the mystification of the masses by culture and religion.... Peak's intellectual emancipation, his encounter, as it were, with the changing *esprit de corps* of the traditional intellectual is located as a problem of social mobility, of the organicism of that emancipation. [Peak is] compelled to become a self-made man in a world in which self-making is no longer respectable. [His] epistemological ordeal is defined ... as an ideological situation, a process of self-definition by the given terms of the institutions of ideological co-ercion.... the 'theme' of modernism and ... the 'plot' of social mobility ... work in contradiction ... since it is the scientific spirit that enables Peak to perceive his own determinations and to play a game that will exploit them to the full (equally, it is the limitation of his knowledge that makes him play a game that is self-defeating).

Goode also observes that *Born in Exile* is "strictly comparable with *Jude the Obscure* with this difference—that *Born in Exile* is Jude in reverse." Goode argues that Jude moves from theology to knowledge, from marriage to a free family, whereas Peak moves backwards toward convention. "His death in exile ... is not like Jude's a protest against an oppressive system but simply a record of the failure to achieve integration. Both Jude and Peak fight their intellectual battles as a class war, but they fight it in different directions." One of course sees what Goode means, but at this point Jameson's observations about Gissing's curiously radicalizing effects are especially relevant. Jude's protest is, relative to Peak's, ideologically coherent; it is to a degree a conscious protest against the class system (although this already is to simplify the novel). What Peak does is ideologically incoherent, but for that very reason it makes us uneasy with ideology and calls it into question. When Peak mouths Tory values (the values of the traditional intellectual), those values are undermined rather than sustained. Goode, 57–70.

9. Sidwell's friend Sylvia urges her to act on her "feeling" but finds her the next morning in her "retreat on top of the house. Here Sidwell sat in the light and warmth, a glass door wide open to the west, the rays of a brilliant sun softened by curtains which fluttered lightly in the breeze from the sea." Her eyes are turned "to the woody hills on the far side of the Exe" (494). In such a passage we may readily see how much Gissing shares Peak's enthusiasm for the Warricombes' luxury; "rural loveliness" remained a compelling feature of the world of affluent decorum, and it is indicative of Gissing's own "double consciousness" that in his vocabulary, Sidwell's "retreat" refers not to a moral weakness but to a beautiful view.

10. See Trilling on the shift from "sincerity" to "authenticity" or to the "sentiment of being," in *Sincerity and Authenticity,* especially 99–111.

11. Korg, "The Spiritual Theme," 140.

12. Peak's snobbery is part of his effort to establish an identity, to alienate himself from one class so as to be free to join another. His words at all times express not who he is but who he might like to be; they are fragments of a consciousness whose integrity has been shattered by the

decision not to belong to the world in which he was born. In his *Problems of Dostoevsky's Poetics* (Ann Arbor: Ardis, 1973, 150–69), Mikhail Bakhtin coins the term "dialogical speech" to describe the fragmented consciousness of characters like Raskolnikov, the Underground Man, or Stavrogin, whose minds are ideological battlegrounds and who compulsively incorporate into their dialogue and interior monologue the stance of particular interlocutors. We might think of Peak as a cousin-german to such illustrious company, conducting the ideological struggle at the level of social mores and sensibility rather than at the level of ideas. Such a passage as that in which Peak reflects, with tears in his eyes, on the English country home illustrates his "disintegrated consciousness," within which his Tory sensibility and his resentment of the social hierarchy clash. His admiration for the upper-middle class discloses both his lack of integrity and the meanness of his ideal.

13. Gissing, *Demos* (New York: Dutton, n. d.), 350.

14. Jameson argues in his essay on the early novels that Gissing reveals the same kind of resentment that I have detected in Peak. He suggests that certain passages, among them the one I quote from *Demos,* must be analyzed as "dialogical," that is, as speech directed to a listener (here, the middle-class reader) which incorporates the listener's values into the language. Jameson argues that Gissing's

> mimicry of Tory attitudes and upper-class snobbery is somehow blank of all identification: these complacent and intolerable values *somehow express themselves impersonally* without the intervention of authorial subjectivity, or of any real individual commitment. So it is not difficult to detect a deeper level of intention in such passages in which it is precisely a hostility for the dominant classes themselves which finds issue through their imitation; a hostility rewarded by the inevitable embarrassment of genuinely snobbish readers at finding their values thus enthusiastically endorsed by someone who has no right to them... (148, emphasis added).

I doubt whether a stylistic analysis of these earlier novels could prove that "deeper level of intention... hostility for the dominant classes [which] finds issue through their imitation." My italics suggest that Jameson, too, is uncertain of how he can detect this other intention. But the striking aspect of *Born in Exile* is that here Gissing sought to show exactly such an effect in Peak's imitation. The additional turn of the screw in having his own conservative spokesman an imposter strongly suggests that Gissing was deliberately exploring these issues. But to what extent he might have read back the hostility beneath Peak's snobbery into his own reactionary position, as expressed, say, in the passage from *Demos,* is an open question. The notion of "dialogical speech" reminds us that fiction provides a way of knowing and saying things which remain unacceptable or inadmissible to our public selves.

Chapter 2

1. "Wessex Heights," in *The Complete Poems of Thomas Hardy,* James Gibson, ed. (London: Macmillan, 1976), 319. Subsequent quotations of the poetry are from this edition. On interpretation see J. O. Bailey, *The Poetry of Thomas Hardy* (Chapel Hill: University of North Carolina Press, 1970), 181–82; and F. B. Pinion, *A Commentary on the Poems of Thomas Hardy* (New York: Barnes & Noble, 1976), 95–97, 59–60.

2. Thomas Hardy, *The Life and Work of Thomas Hardy,* Michael Millgate, ed. (Athens: University of Georgia Press, 1985), 63. This is a useful new edition of Hardy's ghostwritten autobiography, originally published under his second wife's name as *The Early Life of*

Thomas Hardy: 1840–1891, and *The Later Years of Thomas Hardy: 1892–1928.* References to this edition hereafter will appear in parentheses in the text with the notation LWTH and page number.

3. The most recent and comprehensive biography is Michael Millgate's *Thomas Hardy: A Biography* (New York: Random House, 1982). I have also drawn on Robert Gittings' *Young Thomas Hardy* and *Thomas Hardy's Later Years* (Boston: Little, Brown, 1975 and 1978); hereafter YTH and THLY. Gittings places particular emphasis on Hardy's break with his past. See also Carl Weber's *Hardy of Wessex* (New York: Columbia University Press, 1940. Rev. ed. 1965).

4. Raymond Williams, *The Country and the City* (New York: Oxford University Press, 1973), 197, 210. Irving Howe, *Thomas Hardy* (New York: Macmillan, 1968), 21, 24.

5. Thomas Hardy, *Jude the Obscure,* New Wessex Edition (London: Macmillan, 1974), 97. Subsequent references to this edition appear in parentheses in the text.

6. Gittings, YTH, 198–212.

7. Robert Gittings has argued forcefully that *The Life* was consciously intended to play down the radical nature of Hardy's change in station. "To shut the door on a social past from which he had escaped became a compulsion in his later life," YTH, 4. In his more comprehensive and more recent work Michael Millgate does not deny that Hardy's experience of mobility was stressful throughout most of his life, but he does not see him, as Gittings does, as obsessed with covering up his family history. Millgate stresses the close ties which Hardy maintained with his immediate family and his continuing admiration for his parents' way of life, even though he had chosen not to share it. Characteristic of Millgate's fully rounded portrait of Hardy is the following explanation for the numerous entries about Hardy's social life among the upper-middle class—entries which it would be easy to ascribe to a kind of snobbish name-dropping:

    > In part they must have provided a means of filling out the record of years whose really significant events—the onset of middle-age, the final desolation of his first marriage, the abortive affairs of the heart with other women—were too private and painful for public revelation. In part they must have reflected Hardy's active enjoyment of a world which had at the very least a colour, a glamour … pleasantly at odds with the drabness of his early years. … But it seems equally likely that such social details were supplied for the simple reason that Hardy thought people would be interested in them—interested in his having met Lord Salisbury … rather than in Lord Salisbury's … having met Thomas Hardy (LWTH, xxv).

8. *The Collected Letters of Thomas Hardy,* Richard Little Purdy and Michael Millgate, eds., vol. I (Oxford: Clarendon Press, 1978), 7–8.

9. See J. O. Bailey, "Ancestral Voices in *Jude the Obscure*" in *The Classic British Novel,* H. M. Harper, Jr., and Charles Edge, eds. (Athens, GA: University of Georgia Press, 1972), 152; Gittings, YTH, 46; Bailey, *The Poetry,* 278; Pinion, 361. Gittings points out that "A Bishop of Salisbury (Melchester) is pilloried and made a fool of in *Two on a Tower*." "The Son's Veto" and "A Tragedy of Two Ambitions" both associate churchmen with vicious snobbery.

10. "A Tragedy of Two Ambitions" in *Life's Little Ironies,* XIV of *The Mellstock Edition of The Works of Thomas Hardy* (London: Macmillan, 1920), 85. Subsequent references to this edition are given in parentheses in the text.

11. "The Simpletons," "The Recalcitrants," and "Hearts Insurgent" were alternate titles for *Jude the Obscure;* the first suggests an ironic treatment of the protagonist's idealism while the second and third emphasize the element of social protest. See Richard L. Purdy, *Thomas Hardy: A Bibliographical Study* (Oxford: The Clarendon Press, 1954), 87.

12. In the holograph Jude is first called Jack Head and later Jack Hopeson, Hopson being the maiden name of Mary Head's mother. Bailey in "Ancestral Voices" summarizes many of these autobiographical links. See also Weber, 200–203.

13. On Antell, see Millgate, 107–8, 347–48 and Gittings, THLY, 66 and YTH, 217–18; see YTH, chap. 2, for an account of how Hardy drew on his family's history in his fiction, and THLY, 56–57 on avatars for Tess. See Millgate, chapter 18, for autobiographical material in *Jude.* Both Millgate and Gittings suggest that Horace Moule's character gave Hardy some material for Jude.

14. For instance, in *The Life* (19–20) Hardy describes himself as a young boy in this way.

> He was of ecstatic temperament, extraordinarily sensitive to music, and among the endless jigs . . . there were three or four that always moved the child to tears. . . . This peculiarity in himself troubled [him]. . . . the staircase at Bockhampton . . . had its walls coloured Venetian red by his father, and was so situated that the evening sun shone into it, adding to its colour a great intensity for a quarter of an hour or more. Tommy used to wait for this chromatic effect, and, sitting alone there, would recite to himself "And now another day is gone" from Dr. Watts's Hymns, with great fervency, though perhaps not for any religious reason, but from a sense that the scene suited the lines.

Jude too is a rather sad, weepy little boy. His first sight of Christminster at sunset throws him into a kind of ecstasy, spawned half by his imagination and half by light. Though there is no music in his impoverished world, he is moved by the sight of the moon and the sounds of Horace's verse, like Hardy, "less from any religious reason [than] from a sense that the scene suited the lines." Jude's concern for animals, even worms, reflects Hardy's lifelong and occasionally maudlin tenderness.

15. See the discussion on university education in chapter 1.

16. I am indebted in this analysis to Richard Sennett and Jonathan Cobb, *The Hidden Injuries of Class* (New York: Vintage Books, 1973), especially chapter 3, "The Uses of Injured Dignity."

17. Terry Eagleton's reading of *Jude,* which appears as the introduction to the New Wessex Edition, develops this point. He writes that "the relation between ideal and reality in the novel is dialectical. The more starved and barren actual life is, the more the ideals it generates will be twisted into bodiless illusions. . . ." Eagleton's thesis is essentially my own: "The historical irony in which Jude is trapped is that personal fulfilment can be achieved only by painfully appropriating the very culture which denies and rejects him as a man . . ." (14). I hope that my close reading of some key scenes will add to the persuasiveness of Eagleton's argument.

18. Jean Brooks, *Thomas Hardy: The Poetic Structure* (Ithaca: Cornell University Press, 1971), 254; Albert Guerard, *Thomas Hardy* (New York: New Directions, 1962).

19. Norman Holland, "*Jude the Obscure:* Hardy's Symbolic Indictment of Christianity," *Nineteenth-Century Fiction,* 9 (1954), 50–60.

20. David DeLaura, "'The Ache of Modernism' in Hardy's Later Novels," *English Literary History,* 34 (1967), 380–99; Robert Heilman, "Hardy's Sue Bridehead," *Nineteenth-Century Fiction,* 20 (1966), 307–23.

21. Edmund Gosse's review of *Jude the Obscure* in *Cosmopolis* (January 1896), reprinted in *Thomas Hardy: The Critical Heritage,* R. B. Cox, ed. (New York: Barnes and Noble), 1970, 266.

22. The line of verse is from "Wessex Heights."

Chapter 3

1. The principal biographies are Reginald Pound's *Arnold Bennett: A Biography* (London: Heinemann, 1952) and Margaret Drabble's *Arnold Bennett* (New York: Alfred A. Knopf, 1974). Pound speculates that the experience of an early, shameful poverty may have scarred Bennett in the same way that the experience in the blacking factory scarred Dickens (Pound, 50).

2. The epigraphs for the chapter are from H. G. Wells's *Kipps: The Story of a Simple Soul* (New York: Scribners, 1906) and Arnold Bennett's "Middle Class," in *Books and Persons* (New York: George H. Doran, 1917), 90.

3. Letter to Sturt in *Letters of Arnold Bennett,* vol. 2, James Hepburn, ed. (New York: Oxford University Press, 1968), 12. Sturt's response is found on 20 of the same volume.

4. "The 'Average Reader' and the Recipe for Popularity" is reprinted in *The Author's Craft and Other Critical Writings of Arnold Bennett,* Samuel Hynes, ed. (Lincoln: University of Nebraska Press, 1968). The title essay includes Bennett's comments on the author's need to compromise with the public, to learn to become a "merchant."

5. The phrase is from Arnold Bennett, *The Truth about an Author* (New York: George H. Doran, 1911), 65.

6. Denry Machin, the hero of *The Card,* is born on Bennett's birthday. The son of a poor seamstress in Bursley, Denry wins a place in the Grammar School by forging his academic record and is eventually apprenticed to a solicitor. From then on he wheels and deals, with only minor illegalities and a great deal of chutzpah, to the top of Bursley society and from there he moves eventually to Switzerland.

7. *Clayhanger* is the first novel in *The Clayhanger Trilogy;* Bennett apparently conceived of the idea of a trilogy while writing *Clayhanger. Hilda Lessways* was published in 1911, *These Twain* in 1915. The rationale for treating the novel essentially independently of the trilogy is that it is widely regarded as the best of the three, standing apart in tone and quality.

8. Georg Lukács, *The Theory of the Novel,* Anna Bostock, trans. (Cambridge: The M.I.T. Press, 1971), 136; the subsequent quotation is from 137. The discussion of the Bildungsroman is on 132–43.

9. A journal entry for 15 October 1896, in *The Journal of Arnold Bennett 1896–1910* (New York: Viking Press, 1932), 22.

10. The quotation from Walter Allen is in *The English Novel* (New York: E. P. Dutton, 1954), 387. A particularly fine short story, "The Death of Simon Fuge," explores the necessity for the artist to leave home; it is in the collection *The Grim Smile of the Five Towns.* See John Lucas, *Arnold Bennett: A Study of His Fiction* (London: Methuen, 1974), 91–94, for an excellent discussion of this theme. The phrase "the Usual . . . transformed by Art into the Sublime" is from *The Truth about an Author,* 65. While much of the work is a spoof, this passage seems to express Bennett's own esthetic.

11. *Journal,* 30.

12. Bennett, *A Man from the North,* chap. 12, quoted in Lucas, 20.

13. Bennett, "The Author's Craft," 8–9.

14. The phrase is from *Clayhanger* (New York: Penguin Books, 1954. Reprint 1976), 30. There is no standard edition of Bennett's novels so I have used a widely available paperback edition; subsequent references to this edition appear in parentheses in the text.

15. As he was correcting the galley proofs for *Clayhanger* Bennett noted "the far too frequent use of the world 'extraordinary,' but I hadn't sufficient interest to suppress it occasionally in correcting" (*Journal,* 388). I question whether such uncharacteristic neglect of craftsmanship was due to genuine apathy; it might be read as an indication of his continuing uncertainty about his attitude to his subject matter.

16. The Penguin edition is corrupt, giving "...holy flame of the desire for *self-protection* blazing...." I have corrected this according to the edition published by George H. Doran (New York, 1910).

17. Seeing the clog-dancer was an event of some significance for Bennett, who made the following entry in his *Journal* (349), when visiting Burslem in December, 1909, while he was working up material for *Clayhanger.*

> After dinner I went to the Grand Theatre.... I was profoundly struck by all sorts of things. In particular by the significance of clog-dancing, which had never occurred to me before. I saw a "short study" for *The Nation* in this. Towards the end I came across Warwick Savage and walked home with him. This was a pity because I had got into an extraordinary vein of "second sight." I perceived whole chapters. Of all the stuff I made sufficient notes.

18. *These Twain* (New York: Penguin Books, 1975), 416. The subsequent quotation is from 260.

19. Lucas, 162. His discussion of *These Twain* is from 151–65.

Chapter 4

1. D. H. Lawrence, "Climbing Up," *The Complete Poems,* vol. I, Vivian de Sola Pinto and Warren Roberts, eds. (New York: Viking Press, 1964), 549.

2. Both sketches are reprinted in *Phoenix II: Uncollected, Unpublished, and Other Prose Works* by D. H. Lawrence, ed. by Warren Roberts and Harry T. Moore (New York: Viking Press, 1968), 300–2 and 592–96. As the sketches date from about the same time and are similar in tone and content, I have quoted from both without making any distinctions between them.

3. My approach to Lawrence has much in common with that of Scott Sanders in *D. H. Lawrence: The World of the Five Major Novels* (New York: Viking Press, 1973), Peter Scheckner in *Class, Politics, and the Individual: A Study of the Major Works of D. H. Lawrence* (Rutherford, NJ: Fairleigh Dickinson University Press, 1985) and Graham Holderness in *D. H. Lawrence: History, Ideology and Fiction* (Atlantic Highlands, NJ: Humanities Press, 1982). These critics relate Lawrence's art and thought to his class situation and to the tension between working-class and bourgeois ideology. Holderness in particular provides valuable, detailed information on the ideological conflicts that characterized the world of Lawrence's youth. Terry Eagleton alludes to the issue of the ideological conflict represented in Lawrence's parents in his remarks on the writer in *Criticism and Ideology: A*

Study in Marxist Literary Theory (London: Verso, 1978), 157–60. A longer discussion of the oedipal and social themes in *Sons and Lovers* is in *Literary Theory: An Introduction* (Minneapolis: University of Minnesota Press, 1983), 174–79.

4. V. S. Pritchett, *Sons and Lovers* in *The Living Novel and Later Appreciations* (New York: Random House, 1964), 188.

5. The standard biographies include Harry T. Moore, *The Priest of Love: A Life of D. H. Lawrence* (New York: Farrar, Straus and Giroux, 1974); Edward Nehls, ed., *D. H. Lawrence: A Composite Biography* (Madison: University of Wisconsin Press, 1957); and Emile Delavenay, *D. H. Lawrence: The Man and His Work: The Formative Years: 1885-1919*, trans. K. M. Delavenay (Carbondale: Southern Illinois University Press, 1972). In the "Autobiographical Sketch," Lawrence says of *Sons and Lovers* "the first part is all autobiography." Unlike Paul Morel, Lawrence at thirteen won a scholarship to Nottingham High School for three years. After a few months as a clerk, he contracted pneumonia and had to leave work. He decided to become a teacher and began pupil-teaching in Eastwood while studying on his own. Based on his very high showing in the national King's Scholarship Examination in 1904, he won a scholarship to Nottingham University College where he did a two-year degree which gave him a teaching certificate. He taught at the Davidson School in Croydon from 1908 to November 1911, when at twenty-six he had a second bout of pneumonia and quit teaching. By this time his first novel and several stories and poems had been published and he was able to begin his career as a writer.

6. See chapter 1, "Of Poppies and Phoenixes and the Beginning of the Argument," in *Study of Thomas Hardy, Phoenix: The Posthumous Papers of D. H. Lawrence,* Edward D. McDonald, ed. (London: William Heinemann, 1936. Reprint 1961). Reprinted courtesy of Laurence Pollinger Ltd. and the Estate of Mrs. Frieda Lawrence Ravagli. "The final aim of every living thing, creature, or being is the full achievement of itself.... And I know that the common wild poppy has achieved so far its complete poppy-self...." (403).

7. *Sons and Lovers* (New York: Penguin Books, 1976), 51. Subsequent references to this work will appear in parentheses in the text.

8. In *The Rainbow* (New York: Penguin Books, 1976. Reprint 1981) Ursula thinks of herself as "a princess of Poland" who is under a spell in England (266), much as Miriam thinks of herself as a "swine-girl" who is really a princess. Both are Rapunzels dreaming away in a high tower. For Miriam religion merges with romantic literature: "Christ and God ... Ediths, and Lucys, and Rowenas, Brian de Bois Guilberts, Rob Roys, and Guy Mannerings rustled the sunny leaves in the morning [as she] sat in her bedroom aloft, alone.... that was life to her" (142). Similarly Ursula at twelve

> craved for some spirituality and stateliness. She was just coming to the stage when Andersen and Grimm were being left behind for the "Idylls of the King" and romantic love-stories.... How she leaned in her bedroom window ... the lonely maid high up and isolated in the tower ... always remote and high. (266)

Subsequent references to this edition of *The Rainbow* will appear in parentheses in the text.

9. "A Modern Lover," *The Complete Short Stories*, vol. I (New York: Viking Press, 1973), 5. "The Shades of Spring," originally published as "The Soiled Rose," is also in vol. I. Subsequent references to these works will appear in parentheses in the text. These stories and in particular the variants in the several versions are thoughtfully discussed in Keith Sagar's " 'The Best I have Known': D. H. Lawrence's 'A Modern Lover' and 'The Shades of Spring' "

in *Studies in Short Fiction,* 4 (1967), 144–51; and in Keith Cushman's *D. H. Lawrence at Work: The Emergence of the Prussian Officer Stories* (Charlottesville: University Press of Virginia, 1978).

10. The character's name, John Addington Syson, links him to the homosexual esthete, John Addington Symonds. In "A Modern Lover" Lawrence mentions that Cyril is attractive to the men on the farm and that he is himself attracted to Vickers. Both stories thus question the masculinity of the protagonist, suggesting this is another cause for the failure of the relationship with the girl.

11. Delavenay (121–22) argues that the themes of oedipal attachment and the mother's influence over her sons seemed clearer to Lawrence, once he had completed the novel, that "they actually appear from a reading of the work itself." Lawrence's interpretation

> lends the novel unity... but... fails to take into account the full complexity of the circumstances which... forced Lawrence and Jessie into a platonic friendship.... The over-simple argument discovered by Lawrence after the event, the "split" produced by filial love, does not contain the whole truth; reality is more complex than this Freudian view and includes other aspects of his personality, in particular his sense of having risen above his Nottingham surroundings.

12. A letter of Lawrence's written shortly before his mother's death suggests how aware he was of their suffocating relationship: "Nobody can have the soul of me. My mother has had it, and nobody can have it again. Nobody can come into my very self again, and breathe me like an atmosphere." *The Letters of D. H. Lawrence,* vol. I, James T. Boulton, ed. (Cambridge: Cambridge University Press, 1979) 190–91. Reprinted courtesy of Laurence Pollinger Ltd. and the Estate of Mrs. Frieda Lawrence Ravagli.

13. The letter to Garnett on November 19, 1912, is in *The Letters,* vol. I, 476. Delavenay, 122.

14. *The Letters of D. H. Lawrence,* vol. II, George J. Zytaruk and James T. Boulton, eds. (Cambridge: Cambridge University Press, 1981), 183.

15. Delavenay, 167–69.

16. From "The Song of a Man Who Has Come Through," *The Complete Poems,* 250.

17. Arnold Kettle, *An Introduction to the English Novel,* vol. II (London: Hutchinson University Library, 1974), 108.

18. I have borrowed the idea of dialogic narration in Lawrence from Avrom Fleishman's stimulating essay on *St. Mawr,* "He Do the Polis in Different Voices: Lawrence's Later Style" in *D. H. Lawrence: A Centenary Consideration,* Peter Balbert and Phillip L. Marcus, eds. (Ithaca: Cornell University Press, 1985), 162–79. Fleishman adopts the term "dialogical narrative" from Mikhail Bakhtin.

19. Scott Sanders discusses the similarity between Lawrence's depiction of nature and industrial society. Both are impersonal, autonomous forces over which the individual has no control. The image of nature "outlines a projection of the experience of society. The reified natural process corresponds to the reified social process.... The less control men had over their life in society—particularly those men who, like Lawrence, were unable to commit themselves to any collective action, and thereby to merge their individuality into the group—the greater their need to believe in some autonomous realm, perhaps of nature, which would remain immune to the pressures of history" (57).

20. *The Letters,* vol. II, 183.

21. "Democracy," in *Phoenix,* 715. Compare a passage in which Birkin expresses similar sentiments in *Women in Love* (New York: Penguin Books, 1960), 115.

22. *Phoenix,* 587–668.

Conclusion

1. Eagleton, *Literary Theory,* 172.

2. It is a little startling to recognize in Masterman, the socialist, a partial portrait of Wells's friend George Gissing. His consumptive lungs and black melancholy are recognizable; so also is the contempt for a degraded philistine civilization, out of which the imperative for a socialist revolution emerges.

Bibliography

Allen, Walter. *The English Novel.* New York: E. P. Dutton, 1954.

Althusser, Louis. "Ideology and Ideological State Apparatuses" in *Lenin and Philosophy,* translated by Ben Brewster. London: New Left Books, 1971.

Annan, Noel G. "The Intellectual Aristocracy." In *Studies in Social History,* edited by J. H. Plumb. London: Longmans, Green, 1955.

Arnold, Matthew. *The Complete Prose Works,* 11 vols., edited by R. H. Super. Ann Arbor: University of Michigan Press, 1960–1977.

Bailey, J. O. "Ancestral Voices in *Jude the Obscure.*" In *The Classic British Novel,* edited by H. M. Harper, Jr. and Charles Edge. Athens: University of Georgia Press, 1972.

_____. *The Poetry of Thomas Hardy.* Chapel Hill: University of North Carolina Press, 1970.

Bakhtin, Mikhail. *The Dialogic Imagination: Four Essays,* edited by Michael Holquist, translated by Caryl Emerson and Michael Holquist. Austin: University of Texas Press, 1981.

_____. *Problems of Dostoyevsky's Poetics,* translated by R. W. Rotsel. Ann Arbor: Ardis, 1973.

Balbert, Peter and Phillip L. Marcus, eds. *D. H. Lawrence: A Centenary Consideration.* Ithaca: Cornell University Press, 1985.

Batchelor, John. *The Edwardian Novelists.* New York: St. Martin's Press, 1982.

Bennett, Arnold. *Anna of the Five Towns.* New York: Penguin Books, 1978.

_____. *The Author's Craft and Other Critical Writings,* edited by Samuel Hynes. Lincoln: University of Nebraska Press, 1968.

_____. *Books and Persons.* New York: George H. Doran, 1917.

_____. *Clayhanger.* New York: Penguin Books, 1954, reprint 1976 and New York: George H. Doran, 1910.

_____. *Denry the Audacious.* (American title for *The Card*). New York: Dutton, 1911.

_____. *The Grim Smile of the Five Towns.* New York: Penguin Books, 1985.

_____. *Hilda Lessways.* New York: Penguin Books, 1975, reprint 1976.

_____. *The Journal of Arnold Bennett.* 3 vols. New York: Viking, 1932.

_____. *The Letters of Arnold Bennett,* 3 vols., edited by James Hepburn. London: Oxford University Press, 1966–1970.

_____. *A Man from the North.* Salem, NH: Ayer, 1976.

_____. *The Old Wives' Tale.* New York: Penguin Books, 1983.

_____. *The Truth about an Author.* New York: George H. Doran, 1911.

_____. *These Twain.* New York: Penguin Books, 1975, reprint 1976.

Berger, Milton M., ed. *Beyond the Double Bind: Communication and Family Systems, Theories, and Techniques with Schizophrenics.* New York: Brunner/Mazel, 1978.

Best, Geoffrey. *Mid-Victorian Britain: 1851–1875.* London: Weidenfeld and Nicolson, 1971.

Boumelha, Penny. *Thomas Hardy and Women: Sexual Ideology and Narrative Form.* Totowa, NJ: Barnes and Noble, 1982.

Brooks, Jean. *Thomas Hardy: The Poetic Structure.* Ithaca: Cornell University Press, 1971.

Broomfield, Olga R. R. *Arnold Bennett.* Boston: G. K. Hall, 1984.

Buckley, Jerome Hamilton. *Season of Youth: The Bildungsroman from Dickens to Golding.* Cambridge: Harvard University Press, 1974.

Burns, Elizabeth and Tom. *Sociology of Literature and Drama.* Harmondsworth: Penguin, 1973.

Casagrande, Peter J. *Unity in Hardy's Novels: "Repetitive Symmetries."* Lawrence: University of Kansas Press, 1982.

Caudwell, Christopher. *Studies and Further Studies in a Dying Culture.* New York: Monthly Review Press, 1971.

Clark, G. Kitson. *The Making of Victorian England.* Cambridge: Harvard University Press, 1962.

Clarke, Colin, ed. *D. H. Lawrence: The Rainbow and Women in Love.* Nashville: Aurora, 1970.

Collie, Michael. *The Alien Art: A Critical Study of George Gissing's Novels.* Hamden, CT: Archon Books, 1979.

Coustillas, Pierre, ed. *Collected Articles on George Gissing.* New York: Barnes and Noble, 1970.

————. "Introduction" to *Born in Exile.* Sussex: Harvester Press, 1978.

————, ed. *London and the Life of Literature in Late Victorian England: The Diary of George Gissing, Novelist.* Lewisburg: Bucknell University Press, 1978.

Cox, G. Stevens. "Some Notes on '*Jude the Obscure,*' Thomas Hardy and Oxford." In *Thomas Hardy Yearbook* (1972–73), 40–43.

Cox, R. G., ed. *Thomas Hardy: The Critical Heritage.* New York: Barnes and Noble, 1970.

Cushman, Keith. *D. H. Lawrence at Work: The Emergence of the Prussian Officer Stories.* Charlottesville: University Press of Virginia, 1978.

Daleski, H. M. *The Forked Flame: A Study of D. H. Lawrence.* Evanston: Northwestern University Press, 1965.

DeLaura, David J. "'The Ache of Modernism' in Hardy's Later Novels." *English Literary History,* 34 (1967), 380–99.

Delavenay, Emile. *D. H. Lawrence: The Man and His Work: The Formative Years: 1885–1919,* translated by K. M. Delavenay. Carbondale: Southern Illinois University Press, 1972.

Donnelly, Mabel Collins. *George Gissing: Grave Comedian.* Cambridge: Harvard University Press, 1954.

Drabble, Margaret. *Arnold Bennett.* New York: Alfred A. Knopf, 1974.

Eagleton, Terry. *Criticism and Ideology: A Study in Marxist Literary Theory.* London: New Left Books, Verso Edition, 1978.

————. *Literary Theory: An Introduction.* Minneapolis: University of Minnesota Press, 1983.

————. *Marxism and Literary Criticism.* Berkeley: University of California Press, 1976.

————. *Myths of Power: A Marxist Study of the Brontës.* New York: Barnes and Noble, 1975.

Ensor, R. C. K. *England: 1870–1914.* In the Oxford History of England Series, edited by G. N. Clark. Oxford: Clarendon Press, 1936.

Ford, George H. *Double Measure: A Study of the Novels and Stories of D. H. Lawrence.* New York: Norton, 1965.

Forster, E. M. *Howards End.* New York: Vintage Books, 1958.

————. *Two Cheers for Democracy.* New York: Harcourt, Brace and World, 1951.

Friedman, Alan. *The Turn of the Novel.* New York: Oxford University Press, 1966.

Giordano, Frank R. "*Jude the Obscure* and the Bildungsroman." In *Studies in the Novel,* 4 (1972), 580–91.

Gissing, George. *Born in Exile.* Sussex: Harvester Press, 1978.

————. *Demos.* New York: E. P. Dutton, n. d.

————. *New Grub Street.* Boston: Houghton Mifflin, 1962.

————. *The Odd Women.* London: Doughty Library Series, 1968.

————. *The Private Papers of Henry Ryecroft.* New York: New American Library, 1961.

———. *Thyrza*. New York: E. P. Dutton, n. d.

———. *The Unclassed*. Sussex: Harvester Press, 1976, reprint 1983.

Gittings, Robert. *Thomas Hardy's Later Years*. Boston: Little, Brown, 1978.

———. *Young Thomas Hardy*. Boston: Little, Brown, 1975.

Goldmann, Lucien. *The Hidden God: A Study of Tragic Vision in the Pensées of Pascal and the Tragedies of Racine*. New York: Humanities Press, 1964.

———. "The Sociology of Literature: Status and Problems of Method," *International Journal of Social Science,* 19 (1967), 493–516.

———. *Towards a Sociology of the Novel*. London: Routledge and Kegan Paul, 1975.

Goode, John. *George Gissing: Ideology and Fiction*. New York: Harper and Row, 1979.

Goodheart, Eugene. *The Utopian Vision of D. H. Lawrence*. Chicago: University of Chicago Press, 1963.

Gregor, Ian. *The Great Web: The Form of Hardy's Major Fiction*. London: Faber and Faber, 1975.

Guerard, Albert, J. *Thomas Hardy*. New York: New Directions, 1962.

Hall, James. *Arnold Bennett: Primitivism and Taste*. Seattle: University of Washington Press, 1959.

Halperin, John. *Gissing: A Life in Books*. New York: Oxford University Press, 1982.

Hamalian, Leo, ed. *D. H. Lawrence: A Collection of Criticism*. New York: McGraw-Hill, 1973.

Hardy, Evelyn. *Thomas Hardy: A Critical Biography*. London: Hogarth, 1954.

Hardy, Thomas. *Collected Letters*, vols. I-V, edited by Richard Little Purdy and Michael Millgate. Oxford: Clarendon Press, 1978–85.

———. *The Complete Poems*, edited by James Gibson. London: Macmillan, 1976.

———. *Jude the Obscure*. London: Macmillan, 1974.

———. *The Life and Work of Thomas Hardy*, edited by Michael Millgate. Athens: University of Georgia Press, 1985. An edition of materials previously published over the name of Florence Emily Hardy as *The Early Life of Thomas Hardy: 1840–1891* and *The Later Years of Thomas Hardy: 1892–1928*.

———. *Works*. Mellstock Edition. 37 vols. London: Macmillan, 1919–1920.

Heilman, Robert B. "Hardy's Sue Bridehead." In *Nineteenth-Century Fiction,* 20 (1966), 307–23.

Hellstrom, Ward. "Hardy's Scholar-Gipsy." In *The English Novel in the Nineteenth Century,* edited by George Goodin. Urbana: University of Illinois Press, 1970.

Hicks, Granville. *Figures of Transition: A Study of British Literature at the End of the Nineteenth Century*. New York: Macmillan, 1939.

Hirsch, Marianne. "The Novel of Formation as Genre: Between Great Expectations and Lost Illusions" in *Genre,* 12 (1979), 293–311.

Hochman, Baruch. *Another Ego: The Changing View of Self and Society in the Work of D. H. Lawrence*. Columbia: University of South Carolina Press, 1970.

Hoggart, Richard. *The Uses of Literacy: Changing Patterns in English Mass Culture*. Boston: Beacon Press, 1961.

Holderness, Graham. *D. H. Lawrence: History, Ideology and Fiction*. Atlantic Highlands, NJ: Humanities Press, 1982.

Holland, Norman. "*Jude the Obscure:* Hardy's Symbolic Indictment of Christianity." In *Nineteenth-Century Fiction,* 9 (1954), 50–60.

Holloway, John. *The Victorian Sage*. New York: Norton, 1965.

Houghton, Walter E. *The Victorian Frame of Mind: 1830–1870*. New Haven: Yale University Press, 1957.

Howard, David B., et al., eds. *Tradition and Tolerance in Nineteenth-Century Fiction*. New York: Barnes and Noble, 1967.

Howe, Irving. *Thomas Hardy*. New York: Macmillan, 1968.

Howe, Susanne. *Wilhelm Meister and His English Kinsmen.* New York: Columbia University Press, 1950.

Hynes, Samuel. *The Edwardian Turn of Mind.* Princeton: Princeton University Press, 1968.

Jackson, Holbrook. *The Eighteen Nineties.* London: Jonathan Cape, 1913.

James, Henry. *The Princess Casamassima.* New York: Harper and Row, 1968.

Jameson, Fredric. "Authentic *Ressentiment:* The 'Experimental' Novels of Gissing." In *Nineteenth-Century Fiction,* 31 (1976), 127–49.

――――. *Marxism and Form: Twentieth-Century Dialectical Theories of Literature.* Princeton: Princeton University Press, 1971.

――――. *The Political Unconscious: Narrative as a Socially Symbolic Act.* Ithaca: Cornell University Press, 1981.

Kermode, Frank. *D. H. Lawrence.* New York: Viking Press, 1973.

Kettle, Arnold. *An Introduction to the English Novel,* 2 vols. London: Hutchinson University Library, 1974.

Kinkead-Weeks, Mark, ed. *Twentieth Century Interpretations of The Rainbow.* Englewood Cliffs: Prentice-Hall, 1971.

Knickerbocker, William S. "Victorian Education and the Idea of Culture." In *The Reinterpretation of Victorian Literature,* edited by Joseph E. Baker. New York: Russell and Russell, 1962.

Korg, Jacob. *George Gissing: A Critical Biography.* Seattle: University of Washington Press, 1963.

Lang, Berel and Forrest Williams. *Marxism and Art: Writings in Aesthetics and Criticism.* New York: David McKay, 1972.

Laurenson, Diana T. and Alan Swingewood. *The Sociology of Literature.* New York: Schocken Books, 1972.

Lawrence, D. H. *The Complete Poems,* 2 vols., edited by Vivian de Sola Pinta and Warren Roberts, New York: Viking Press, 1964.

――――. *The Complete Short Stories,* 3 vols. New York: Viking Press, 1961.

――――. *Lady Chatterley's Lover.* New York: Bantam Books, 1971.

――――. *The Letters,* vol. I, edited by James T. Boulton. Cambridge: Cambridge University Press, 1979. Vol. II, edited by George J. Zytaruk and James T. Boulton, 1981.

――――. *Phoenix: The Posthumous Papers,* edited by Edward D. McDonald. London: Heinemann, 1936, reprint 1961.

――――. *Phoenix II: Uncollected, Unpublished, and Other Prose Works,* edited by Warren Roberts and Harry T. Moore. New York: Viking Press, 1968.

――――. *The Rainbow.* New York: Penguin Books, 1976, reprint 1981.

――――. *Sons and Lovers.* New York: Penguin Books, 1976.

――――. *Women in Love.* New York: Penguin Books, 1960.

Leavis, F. R. *D. H. Lawrence: Novelist.* New York: Simon and Schuster, 1969.

Lucas, John. *Arnold Bennett: A Study of His Fiction.* London: Methuen, 1974.

――――. *Literature and Politics in the Nineteenth Century.* London: Methuen, 1971.

Lukács, Georg. *Studies in European Realism.* New York: Grosset and Dunlap, 1974.

――――. *The Theory of the Novel,* translated by Anna Bostock. Cambridge: The MIT Press, 1971.

Macherey, Pierre. *A Theory of Literary Production,* translated by Geoffrey Wall. London: Routledge and Kegan Paul, 1978.

McPherson, Robert G. *Theory of Higher Education in Nineteenth-Century England.* University of Georgia Monographs, no. 4. Athens: University of Georgia Press, 1959.

Miller, J. Hillis. *Thomas Hardy: Distance and Desire.* Cambridge: Harvard University Press, 1970.

Millgate, Michael. *Thomas Hardy: A Biography.* New York: Random House, 1982.

――――. *Thomas Hardy: His Career as a Novelist.* New York: Random House, 1971.

Mizener, Arthur. "*Jude the Obscure* as a Tragedy." *Southern Review,* 6 (1949), 193–213.

Moore, Harry T. *The Priest of Love: A Life of D. H. Lawrence.* New York: Farrar, Straus and Giroux, 1974.

Mountford, James. *British Universities.* London: Oxford University Press, 1966.

Nehls, Edward, ed. *D. H. Lawrence: A Composite Biography.* Madison: University of Wisconsin Press, 1957.

Newton, Judith Lowder. *Women, Power, and Subversion: Social Strategies in British Fiction, 1778–1860.* Athens: University of Georgia, 1981.

Orel, Harold, ed. *Thomas Hardy's Personal Writings.* Lawrence: University of Kansas Press, 1966.

Page, Norman, ed. *Thomas Hardy: The Writer and His Background.* New York: St. Martin's Press, 1980.

Pinion, F. B. *A Commentary on the Poems of Thomas Hardy.* New York: Barnes and Noble, 1976.

––––––. *A Hardy Companion: A Guide to the Works of Thomas Hardy and Their Background.* New York: St. Martin's Press, 1968.

––––––. *Thomas Hardy: Art and Thought.* Totowa, NJ: Rowman and Littlefield, 1977.

Poole, Adrian. *Gissing in Context.* Totowa, NJ: Rowman and Littlefield, 1975.

Poovey, Mary. *The Proper Lady and the Woman Writer: Ideology as Style in the Works of Mary Wollstonecraft, Mary Shelley, and Jane Austen.* Chicago: University of Chicago Press, 1984.

Pound, Reginald. *Arnold Bennett: A Biography.* London: Heinemann, 1952.

Pritchett, V. S. *The Living Novel and Later Appreciations.* New York: Random House, 1964.

Proctor, Mortimer R. *The English University Novel.* English Studies: 15. Berkeley: University of California Press, 1957.

Purdy, Richard L. *Thomas Hardy: A Bibliographical Study.* Oxford: Clarendon Press, 1954.

Rice, Thomas Jackson. *D. H. Lawrence: A Guide to Research.* New York: Garland, 1983.

Sagar, Keith. *The Art of D. H. Lawrence.* Cambridge: Cambridge University Press, 1966.

––––––. "'The Best I Have Known': D. H. Lawrence's 'A Modern Lover' and 'The Shades of Spring.'" In *Studies in Short Fiction,* 4 (1967), 144–51.

––––––. *D. H. Lawrence: A Calendar of His Works.* Austin: University of Texas Press, 1979.

Sanders, Scott. *D. H. Lawrence: The World of the Five Major Novels.* New York: Viking Press, 1974.

Scheckner, Peter. *Class, Politics, and the Individual: A Study of the Major Works of D. H. Lawrence.* Rutherford, NJ: Fairleigh Dickinson University Press, 1985.

Selig, Robert L. *George Gissing.* Boston: G. K. Hall, 1983.

Sennett, Richard and Jonathan Cobb. *The Hidden Injuries of Class.* New York: Vintage Books, 1973.

Simon, Brian. *Studies in the History of Education: 1780–1870.* London: Lawrence and Wishart, 1969.

Slack, Robert C. "The Text of Hardy's *Jude the Obscure.*" In *Nineteenth-Century Fiction,* 11 (1957), 251–75.

Smith, Peter. *Public and Private Value: Studies in the Nineteenth-Century Novel.* Cambridge: Cambridge University Press, 1984.

Spacks, Patricia Meyer. *The Adolescent Idea: Myths of Youth and the Adult Imagination.* New York: Basic Books, 1981.

Spilka, Mark, ed. *D. H. Lawrence: A Collection of Critical Essays.* Englewood Cliffs: Prentice-Hall, 1963.

Stange, G. Robert. "Introduction." *The History of Henry Esmond, Esq.* By W. M. Thackeray. New York: Holt, Rinehart, and Winston, 1962.

Stewart, J. I. M. *Thomas Hardy: A Critical Biography.* New York: Dodd, Mead and Co., 1971.

Stone, Donald David. *Novelists in a Changing World.* Cambridge: Harvard University Press, 1972.

Stone, Lawrence, ed., *The University in Society,* vol. 1, *Oxford and Cambridge from the Fourteenth to the Early Nineteenth Century.* Princeton: Princeton University Press, 1974.

Stone, Lawrence and Jeanne C. Fawtier Stone. "Literacy and Education in England: 1640–1900," in *Past and Present,* 42 (1969), 69–139.

———. *An Open Elite? England 1540–1880.* Oxford: Clarendon Press, 1984.

Swales, Martin. *The German Bildungsroman from Wieland to Hesse.* Princeton: Princeton University Press, 1978.

Swingewood, Alan. *The Novel and Revolution.* London: Macmillan, 1975.

Talbott, J. E. "Education in Intellectual and Social History." In *Historical Studies Today,* edited by Felix Gilbert and Stephen R. Graubard. New York: Norton, 1971, 193–210.

Tedlock. E. W., Jr., ed. *D. H. Lawrence and Sons and Lovers: Sources and Criticism.* New York: New York University Press, 1965.

Tennyson, G. B. "The *Bildungsroman* in Nineteenth-Century English Literature." In *Medieval Epic to the 'Epic Theater' of Brecht,* edited by R. P. Armato and J. M. Spalek. Los Angeles: University of California Press, 1968.

Thompson, E. P. *The Making of the English Working Class.* New York: Penguin Books, 1968.

Tindall, Gillian. *The Born Exile.* New York: Harcourt, Brace and Jovanovich, 1974.

Trilling, Lionel. *Matthew Arnold.* New York: Columbia University Press, 1949.

———. *Sincerity and Authenticity.* Cambridge: Harvard University Press, 1971.

Vivas, Eliseo. *D. H. Lawrence: The Failure and Triumph of Art.* Evanston: Northwestern University Press, 1960.

Voss, James. "Arnold Bennett's Realism: Social Process and the Individual in *Anna of the Five Towns*" in *Orbis Litterarum,* 38 (1983), 168–84.

Wain, John. *Arnold Bennett.* New York: Columbia University Press, 1967.

Watt, Ian. *The Rise of the Novel.* Berkeley: University of California Press, 1965.

Weber, Carl. *Hardy of Wessex.* New York: Columbia University Press, 1940.

Wells, H. G. *Kipps: The Story of a Simple Soul.* New York: Scribners, 1906.

———. *Tono-Bungay.* New York: New American Library, 1960.

Williams, Merryn. *Thomas Hardy and Rural England.* New York: Columbia University Press, 1972.

Williams, Raymond. *The Country and the City.* London: Oxford University Press, 1973.

———. *Culture and Society: 1780–1950.* New York: Columbia University Press, 1958, reprint Harper and Row, 1966.

———. *The English Novel from Dickens to Lawrence.* London: Oxford University Press, 1970.

———. *Keywords: A Vocabulary of Culture and Society.* London: Oxford University Press, 1976.

———. *Marxism and Literature.* London: Oxford University Press, 1977.

———. *Writing in Society.* London: New Left Books, Verso Editions, 1983.

Index

Arnold, Matthew: conception of culture as separate from issues of mobility and class, 8–9, 129; influence on *Jude the Obscure*, 57–58

Austen, Jane, 2

Bennett, Arnold: autobiographical material in the fiction of, 75–76, 89; class background, 9–10, 73–74; double bind created by upward mobility, 10–12; double bind in early fiction, 75–77; esthetic convictions, 74–75, 88–89, 91, 95; influence of French naturalists on, 78–79
Clayhanger: double bind in, 77; ideological contradictions in, 85–86, 88; influence of Arnold on, 81; problem of authorial judgment in, 85–88, 89–92, 94–95; problem of irony in, 78, 82–83; redefinition of culture in, 77, 80, 82–84, 88, 92
Other works: "The Author's Craft," 80; *The Card,* 76; *The Old Wives' Tale,* 77; *These Twain,* 93–94; *The Truth about an Author,* 75

Bildungsroman: and autobiography, 11; contradictions within, 13–14; definition of, 1, 133n1; history of, 1–4; Lukács's study of, 77–78; upward mobility as a theme in, 1–4, 11–12

Brontë, Charlotte, 3

Brooks, Jean, 59

Butler, Samuel, 3

Class-consciousness. *See* Gissing, George: resentment and class-consciousness, Peak's class-consciousness; Hardy, Thomas: resentment and class-consciousness; Hardy, Thomas: *Jude the Obscure:* contradictions in Jude's class-consciousness

Culture: Arnold's redefinition of, 8–9; Bennett's democratic redefinition of, 77, 80, 82–84, 88, 92; and class in Lawrence, 127–28; and class in Wells, 131–32; ideological contradictions within definition of, 9, 11

Delavenay, Emile, 111

Dialogic narration: 13, 91–92; in Gissing, 28–30, 32–33; in Lawrence, 119–20, 144n18

Dickens, Charles, 3, 133n4

Double bind: definition of, 134n5; in Arnold's redefinition of culture, 8–9; in Bennett, 75–77; in *Jude the Obscure,* 57–60; paradigm in *Born in Exile,* 21–22, 27–28, 33, 35–36; of upward mobility, 4–5, 10–12, 129–30

Eagleton, Terry, 14, 133n3, 140n17, 142n3

Education: as brake on mobility, 6–7; history of, in nineteenth-century England, 5–7

Eliot, George, 53, 133n4

Fielding, Henry, 2

Gifford, Emma Lavinia, 40

Gissing, George: class background, 9–10, 17, 19–20; double bind created by upward mobility, 10–12; influence of Arnold, 11; resentment and class-consciousness, 52; use of Bildungsroman, 11–12
Born in Exile: double bind paradigm in, 21–22, 27–28, 33, 35–36; double consciousness of Peak, 26–27, 28–30, 32–33; influence of Arnold in, 24; Peak's class-consciousness, 23, 24, 25, 27, 30, 31–32; problem of authorial distance in, 21, 26–27, 34; semi-autobiographical, 20, 136n4
Other works: Demos, 18, 20, 21,

DATE DUE